Author: Mary Moore

Proofreaders: Rob Farmer and Aasha Shamsuddin

Content Review: Rob Farmer and Aasha Shamsuddin

Editor: Rob Farmer

Published by Adkins & Matchett (UK) Limited – trading as Adkins Matchett & Toy

First edition 2012

Manufactured in United Kingdom

Visit us at or buy online: www.amttraining.com

AMTM1955

Table of contents

Merger modeling and analysis

Introduction

Doing merger analysis can be a daunting task with endless amounts of work involved in building the model and crunching the numbers. In fact, a great deal of valuable information can be gleaned from even a simple set of numbers and assumptions. The decision about how much to do is based on many factors, including how much time you have, but more importantly, on which analytical tools you wish to use in order to assess the deal in question.

Three levels of merger modeling are considered to illustrate and explain the analytical tools that can be used in each case. The levels of merger modeling are:

- Back of the envelope model (allowing basic analysis)
- Quick and dirty model (including some balance sheet data)
- Fully integrated three statement merger model (to do "the works")

Some of the more technical issues that might be encountered are listed below, and are addressed following the fully integrated three statement merger model:

- Noncontrolling interests (NCI)
- Deal date different to year end
- Different year ends
- Goodwill and asset step-ups

As is best practice when modeling, iteration should be turned off so that a warning appears if a circular reference is created. If essential, intentional circular references should be documented and protected.

Each section of this manual can be used in isolation. For example, to build the fully integrated three statement model and analysis, it is not necessary to work through the prior sections.

Download model templates

To work through the cases in this manual using Excel, download the templates and solution files now…

Download model templates and solution files

A set of downloadable files are available so the examples and cases used in this manual can be followed in Excel. The files available are as follows:

- Back of the envelope merger model template.xls
- Back of the envelope merger model template.xls
- Back of the envelope merger model solution.xls
- Quick and dirty merger model template.xls
- Quick and dirty merger model solution.xls
- Fully integrated three statement merger model template.xls
- Fully integrated three statement merger model solution.xls
- Merger modeling issues NCI template.xls
- Merger modeling issues NCI solution.xls
- Merger modeling issues date problems template.xls
- Merger modeling issues date problems solution.xls

Already registered with AMTonline?

Go to: http://onlinelearning.amttraining.com and log in.

Input your course id using the box in the center of the home screen. Your course ID is: 11

Self-enrol by inputting your enrolment key in the box and press "Enrol me". Your enrolment key is: Q8.BanR0

You now have access to all course materials. Click on each file to download.

Not registered with AMTonline?

Go to: http://onlinelearning.amttraining.com and set up a new account by following the instructions given.

Once you are logged in, input your course id using the box in the center of the home screen. Your course ID is: 11

Self-enrol by inputting your enrolment key in the box and press "Enrol me". Your enrolment key is: Q8.BanR0

You now have access to all course materials. Click on each file to download.

Back of the envelope model

Introduction

This is the most basic level of analysis that can be done. It is quick and easy to do mainly because the information required is readily available.

Information required

- Share prices
- Diluted shares outstanding
- Forecast EPS
- Marginal tax rate

Assumptions needed

- Premium paid
- % stock / debt / cash consideration
- Synergies
- Cost of debt

Analysis possible

- EPS accretion / dilution
- Synergies to breakeven
- Relative PEs
- Ownership dilution

Modeling steps

The following are the steps for a back of the envelope merger model. Each step will be dealt with in turn.

1. Calculate equity value and equity purchase price
2. Forecast earnings per share (EPS) and net income
3. Make necessary assumptions
4. Calculate sources and uses of funds
5. Calculate consolidated diluted shares outstanding
6. Calculate consolidated EPS

Offer premium

Use comparable transactions data to decide what is reasonable

Step 1 - calculate equity value and equity purchase price

Market Data	Buyer	Target	
Company name	Buyer	Target	
Ticker	BUY	TGT	
Unaffected share price	22.26	39.11	
DSO	1,489.7	382.5	
Unaffected equity value	33,160.7	14,959.6	Share price * DSO
Offer premium	nm	30.0%	
Offer price	nm	50.84	Share price * (1 + premium)
Equity purchase price	nm	19,447.4	Offer price * DSO

The unaffected equity value is the pre-deal equity value and is often referred to as market capitalization. This is calculated as:

Unaffected share price * diluted shares outstanding

The offer or acquisition price is the share price of the target adjusted for any offer premium as follows:

Unaffected share price * (1 + premium)

The equity purchase price is the price paid to the existing equity shareholders of the target business and should utilize the offer price as follows:

Offer price * diluted shares outstanding

Step 2 - forecast earnings per share (EPS) and net income

Source EPS forecasts for both the buyer and the target and ensure that they are in line with consensus. Use this to calculate forecast net income (in step 6) by multiplying by the diluted shares outstanding.

Step 3 - make necessary assumptions

Assumptions		
Cost of debt pre-tax	6.5%	
Marginal tax rate	37.6%	
Cost of debt post-tax	4.1%	Pre-tax cost * (1 - MTR)
Debt financing %	30.0%	Set at 100%
Stock financing %	70.0%	(1 - Debt financing %)
Synergies pre-tax	200.0	

Remember...

Sources of funds must always equal uses of funds

Step 4 - calculate sources and uses of funds

The use of funds, in a back of the envelope analysis, is simply the amount needed to buy the equity of the target.

The sources of funds will often be split into the percentage raised from new debt and / or equity issued.

Uses of funds		
Equity purchase price	19,447.4	From Step 1
Total uses of funds	**19,447.4**	
Sources of funds		
Debt issued	5,834.2	Plug
Equity issued	13,613.2	Assumption * equity purchase price
Total sources of funds	**19,447.4**	

Pay attention...

It is very easy to use an incorrect share price when calculating the number of shares to be issued - it must be the buyer share price

Step 5 - calculate consolidated diluted shares outstanding

If equity is being issued to do the deal then the consolidated DSO will be bigger than the current standalone DSO of the buyer. Start with the current DSO of the buyer and increase it by the number of shares that must be issued to do the deal. This is calculated by taking the money amount of equity to be issued (from the sources of funds calculation in step 4) and divide it by the buyer share price. This gives the number of shares that will be issued.

Combo Shares Calculation		
BUY DSO pre-deal	1,489.7	From Step 1
No. shares issued	611.6	Equity issued / BUY share price
Combo DSO	**2,101.3**	Sum
Exchange ratio	1.59884	BUY shares issued / TGT shares bought

Finally, this means we can calculate the exchange ratio. This is the number of buyer shares that a target shareholder will receive in exchange for each share in the target company.

$$\frac{\text{Buyer shares issued (from consolidated DSO calculation)}}{\text{Target shares purchased}}$$

Or:

$$\frac{\text{Offer price}}{\text{Buyer share price}} * \text{\% stock financing}$$

Offer price...

The cash per share and the exchange ratio are communicated to the selling shareholders in the offer document

It is generally shown to four or five decimal places and is always communicated to the target shareholders in the offer document. In this case the selling shareholders will receive 1.59884 buyer shares and 15.25 (debt issued / target DSO) in cash for every share sold.

This can be checked easily as follows:

Consideration per share check		
Offer price per share	**50.84**	From Step 1
Stock value per share	35.59	Exchange ratio * BUY share price
Cash per share	15.25	Offer price * % cash consideraton
Total value per share	**50.84**	Sum stock + cash value

Step 6 - calculate consolidated EPS

Consolidation...

Buyer
+
Target
+ / -
deal changes
=
Consolidated

Income Statement Data	Buyer	Target
Sales - Year 1 F	40,758.0	12,583.6
Sales - Year 2 F	42,409.0	13,133.7
EBITDA - Year 1 F	6,249.0	2,343.6
EBITDA - Year 2 F	6,496.0	2,483.8
Diluted EPS - Year 1 F	1.90	3.06
Diluted EPS - Year 2 F	2.05	3.33

Combo EPS Calculations	*Yr 1 E*	*Yr 2 E*	
+ Net income - BUY	2,830.4	3,053.9	EPS * BUY DSO
+ Net income - TGT	1,170.5	1,273.7	EPS * TGT DSO
+ Synergies post-tax	124.8	124.8	Assumption * (1 - MTR)
- Interest expense post-tax	(236.6)	(236.6)	Debt issued * post-tax cost * -1
= Combo net income	3,889.0	4,215.8	BUY NI + TGT NI + / deal changes
Combo EPS	**1.85**	**2.01**	Combo NI / Combo DSO
Buyer EPS	1.90	2.05	From Step 2

This is a consolidation of net income (NI). As with any consolidation the format is:

Buyer NI + Target NI + / - deal changes = Consolidated NI

The NI numbers for the buyer and target can be calculated from the EPS and DSO numbers. The changes to consolidated net income must be identified. For example, the incremental interest created by newly issued debt will decrease consolidated net income, whilst synergies will increase it. Remember net income is a post-tax number, so all deal changes must be done on a post-tax basis. Finally, the consolidated EPS numbers are calculated.

Consolidated net income / consolidated DSO = Consolidated EPS

Merger consequences analysis

Several pieces of critical analysis can be derived from this back of the envelope model, despite its simplicity, including:

- EPS accretion / dilution
- Synergies to breakeven
- Relative PEs and
- Ownership dilution

Merger consequences analysis - EPS accretion / dilution

Deal Analysis	*Yr 1 E*	*Yr 2 E*	
Buyer P/E	11.7 x	10.9 x	BUY share price / BUY EPS
Acquisition P/E	16.6 x	15.3 x	Offer price / TGT EPS
Debt P/E	24.7 x	24.7 x	1 / post-tax cost of debt
EPS acc. / (dil.)	**(2.6%)**	**(2.1%)**	(Combo EPS / BUY EPS) -1
Synergies to break-even	165.6	147.1	(BUY EPS - Combo EPS) * combo DSO / (1 - MTR)
% BUY ownership	70.9%		BUY DSO / Combo DSO

EPS accretion / dilution is widely used in deal analysis. It shows the extent to which EPS will increase or decrease as a result of the deal.

Naturally, it is purely earnings focused, and ignores key items such as the cost of any equity issued. Its narrow focus means that EPS accretion / dilution should not be used in isolation. A deal that is EPS accretive may not necessarily be a good deal. In the case above, there are only two years of analysis where a small dilution is seen in both years. A longer EPS profile would be helpful.

Merger consequences analysis - synergies to breakeven

Breakeven synergies...

It is useful to sanity check how achievable synergies are by using comparable transaction data

This calculates the additional synergies needed to achieve zero EPS accretion / dilution. Building this calculation up in stages, the first stage is to calculate the EPS needed to achieve breakeven. This is:

Buyer standalone EPS - Consolidated EPS

However, it is unusual in the context of a deal to reference synergies on a per share basis so the next stage grosses this up as follows:

(Buyer standalone EPS - Consolidated EPS) * Consolidate DSO

This gives a gross number, based on net income, which is a post-tax number but it is more common to reference pre-tax numbers for synergies so it must be grossed up for tax:

$$\frac{\text{(Buyer standalone EPS - Consolidated EPS) * Consolidate DSO}}{\text{(1 - MTR)}}$$

Finally, if the deal is accretive already then the answer to this calculation is zero. The formula above will give a negative result which is mathematically correct but does not make sense. An easy fix is to wrap this formula within a MAX function which compares it to zero. The final version becomes:

$$\text{MAX}\left[\frac{\text{(Buyer standalone EPS - Consolidated EPS) * Consolidate DSO}}{\text{(1 - MTR)}}, 0\right]$$

This can be stress tested by setting the synergy assumption to zero which means this calculation will give the total synergies to breakeven.

Assumptions		
Cost of debt pre-tax	6.5%	
Marginal tax rate	37.6%	
Cost of debt post-tax	4.1%	Pre-tax cost * (1 - MTR)
Debt financing %	30.0%	Set at 100%
Stock financing %	70.0%	(1 - Debt financing %)
Synergies pre-tax	0.0	Set at zero

Deal Analysis	*Yr 1 E*	*Yr 2 E*	
Buyer P/E	11.7 x	10.9 x	BUY share price / BUY EPS
Acquisition P/E	16.6 x	15.3 x	Offer price / TGT EPS
Debt P/E	24.7 x	24.7 x	1 / post-tax cost of debt
EPS acc. / (dil.)	**(5.7%)**	**(5.0%)**	(Combo EPS / BUY EPS) -1
Synergies to break-even	365.6	347.1	(BUY EPS - Combo EPS) * combo DSO / (1 - MTR)
% BUY ownership	70.9%		BUY DSO / Combo DSO

Next, copy and paste this formula as a value into the synergy assumption. The EPS accretion / dilution calculation should now show a zero value. Below is an example:

Assumptions		
Cost of debt pre-tax	6.5%	
Marginal tax rate	37.6%	
Cost of debt post-tax	4.1%	Pre-tax cost * (1 - MTR)
Debt financing %	30.0%	Set at 100%
Stock financing %	70.0%	(1 - Debt financing %)
Synergies pre-tax	365.6	Copy and paste value

Deal Analysis	*Yr 1 E*	*Yr 2 E*	
Buyer P/E	11.7 x	10.9 x	BUY share price / BUY EPS
Acquisition P/E	16.6 x	15.3 x	Offer price / TGT EPS
Debt P/E	24.7 x	24.7 x	1 / post-tax cost of debt
EPS acc. / (dil.)	**0.0%**	**0.3%**	(Combo EPS / BUY EPS) -1
Synergies to break-even	0.0	0.0	(BUY EPS - Combo EPS) * combo DSO / (1 - MTR)
% BUY ownership	70.9%		BUY DSO / Combo DSO

Remember to undo your stress tests and reset the assumptions to those intended.

Merger consequences analysis - relative PEs

A comparison of the buyer PE and the acquisition PE gives you a quick analysis of the deal. In the simplest situation of a 100% stock or a 100% cash deal with zero synergies, it will give you the same answer as EPS accretion / dilution. Consequently it should always be used as a stress test of the model, at the very least.

The acquisition (or offer) PE gives an indication of the implied return on equity from this investment. It compares the prices being paid with the earnings being bought. If you calculate the inverse you will get the answer in percentage terms rather than multiple terms. In this example, the year 1 acquisition PE is 16.6 x which implies a 6.0% return on equity.

The return on equity should be compared to the cost of equity to establish whether or not it is sufficient. If the financing is all stock the implied cost of equity is provided by the buyer PE. This gives us the market demand in earnings for every $ invested. Again, the inverse of the PE gives this data in percentage terms. In this case, the buyer PE in the first year is 11.7 x which implies a cost of stock financing of 8.5%.

An investment expected to yield 6.0% and financed with financing costing 8.5% is not, on the face of it, a good deal. This is easily seen by comparing the PEs. The buyer PE is lower than the acquisition PE, which means that the cost of raising buyer equity is higher than return expected from the target equity being purchased. The buyer PE needs to be higher than the acquisition PE in order for the deal to be accretive. Since this analysis only uses the standalone numbers then incremental changes, such as synergies, are not taken into account.

If the assumptions are changed to 100% stock financing and zero synergies, the relative PEs and the EPS accretion / dilution give consistent results.

Assumptions		
Cost of debt pre-tax	6.5%	
Marginal tax rate	37.6%	
Cost of debt post-tax	4.1%	Pre-tax cost * (1 - MTR)
Debt financing %	0.0%	Set at zero
Stock financing %	100.0%	(1 - Debt financing %)
Synergies pre-tax	0.0	Set at zero

Deal Analysis	*Yr 1 E*	*Yr 2 E*	
Buyer P/E	11.7 x	10.9 x	BUY share price / BUY EPS
Acquisition P/E	16.6 x	15.3 x	Offer price / TGT EPS
Debt P/E	24.7 x	24.7 x	1 / post-tax cost of debt
EPS acc. / (dil.)	**(10.9%)**	**(10.7%)**	(Combo EPS / BUY EPS) -1
Synergies to break-even	784.4	828.9	(BUY EPS - Combo EPS) * combo DSO / (1 - MTR)
% BUY ownership	63.0%		BUY DSO / Combo DSO

But what if the financing were different? If cash is paid by issuing debt then the cost of financing is the post-tax cost of debt, in this case, 4.1%. This means that if the implied return on equity purchased is 6.0% and it is financed with debt costing 4.1%, it seems to be a viable deal. Running the numbers with 100% debt financing and zero synergies, this is exactly what is seen - an accretive deal.

PE analysis...

If financing is all stock or all debt and synergies are zero then the PE analysis and the EPS accretion / dilution will be consistent... otherwise... check your model to establish why not

Assumptions		
Cost of debt pre-tax	6.5%	
Marginal tax rate	37.6%	
Cost of debt post-tax	4.1%	Pre-tax cost * (1 - MTR)
Debt financing %	100.0%	Set at 100%
Stock financing %	0.0%	(1 - Debt financing %)
Synergies pre-tax	0.0	Set at zero

Deal Analysis	*Yr 1 E*	*Yr 2 E*	
Buyer P/E	11.7 x	10.9 x	BUY share price / BUY EPS
Acquisition P/E	16.6 x	15.3 x	Offer price / TGT EPS
Debt P/E	24.7 x	24.7 x	1 / post-tax cost of debt
EPS acc. / (dil.)	**13.5%**	**15.9%**	(Combo EPS / BUY EPS) -1
Synergies to break-even	0.0	0.0	(BUY EPS - Combo EPS) * combo DSO / (1 - MTR)
% BUY ownership	100.0%		BUY DSO / Combo DSO

It is more common, in the industry, to do this analysis using PEs rather than percentages. To calculate the "debt PE", simply take the inverse of the post-tax cost of debt. In this case this gives a multiple of 24.7 x.

The PE of the financing must be higher than the acquisition PE in order to produce an accretive deal. In this case, the acquisition PE is higher than the buyer PE but lower than the debt PE which implies dilution if 100% equity financing is used but accretion if 100% debt financing is used. When the model is stress tested using these assumptions and zero synergies this is, in fact, what is observed for EPS accretion / dilution. These stress tests should always be done in order to check the model is working as expected.

One final point, this check works very well at the financing extremes (100% stock or 100% debt) but does not predict well when a mix of financing is used. This is the reason why stress testing by changing the assumptions is critical to test the integrity of the model.

In summary:

If the buyer PE > acquisition PE the deal is likely to be accretive
If the buyer PE < acquisition PE the deal is likely to be dilutive
If the debt PE > acquisition PE the deal is likely to be accretive
If the debt PE < acquisition PE the deal is likely to be dilutive

Merger consequences analysis - ownership dilution

This is important when some or all of the consideration is with stock. It shows the extent to which the buyer shareholders are "giving away" their ownership in the business to pay for the deal. The calculation is straightforward:

$$\frac{\text{Buyer DSO standalone}}{\text{Consolidate DSO}}$$

This shows the percentage ownership in the post-deal world. A key question for the deal team is to understand whether this will be acceptable to the buying shareholders.

Quick and dirty model

Introduction

The disadvantage of the back of the envelope merger model is that some of the analytical tools that are available cannot be used because the information is not to hand. Increasing the complexity, by a fraction, enables this to happen without the commitment to a full blown model.

Information required

- Share prices
- Basic shares outstanding
- Options information for buyer and target
- Foreign exchange rate for cross border deals
- Forecast income statement / profit and loss information - at least 3 years
- Marginal tax rate for both buyer and target
- Balance sheet for both buyer and target

Assumptions needed

- Premium paid
- % stock / debt consideration
- Balance sheet cash available
- Synergies
- Cost of debt
- Rate of interest income on balance sheet cash
- Advisory fees

Analysis possible

- EPS accretion / dilution
- Synergies to breakeven
- Relative PEs
- Ownership dilution
- Contribution analysis
- Side by side comparison
- Analysis at various prices
- Return on invested capital
- Premium analysis

Modeling steps

The following are the steps for a quick and dirty merger model. Each step will be dealt with in turn.

1. Gather market data and calculate share prices
2. Calculate diluted shares outstanding (DSO)
3. Gather historical balance sheet data
4. Gather historical and forecast income statement / profit and loss data
5. Calculate valuation information
6. Make assumptions relating to the deal
7. Calculate sources and uses of funds
8. Calculate consolidated DSO
9. Calculate goodwill
10. Consolidate the balance sheet
11. Consolidate the income statement / profit and loss

> **Offer premium**
>
> Use comparable transactions data to decide what is reasonable

Step 1 - gather market data and calculate share prices

In this example, shown below, the deal is cross border. The simplest way to resolve this is to use a single foreign exchange rate and translate all the relevant target numbers using this rate. This restates the target financials to the currency of the buyer without creating any issues with foreign exchange gains and losses. A further simplification is to assume that the deal date is consistent with the latest financial year end (See section called *Deal date different to year end* on page 71).

Market Data			
Company name	Buyer	Target	
Latest historical year end	31 Dec XX	31 Dec XX	
Currency	ECU	NVR	
Transaction date	31 Dec XX		
FX rate	0.9352		
Ticker symbol	BUY	TGT	
Unaffected share price - NVR	nm	31.51	
Unaffected share price - ECU	54.75	29.47	Share price * fx rate
Offer premium	nm	30.0%	
Offer share price - NVR	nm	40.96	Share price * (1 + premium)
Offer share price - ECU	nm	38.31	Offer price * fx rate

Step 2 - calculate diluted shares outstanding (DSO)

This step calculates the number of diluted shares outstanding for both the buyer and target. Stock based compensation is the most common item to include in these calculations. Most of this is represented by stock options but increasingly other share based compensation, such as restricted stock units, should be included. Restricted stock units are treated as if they were options with a zero strike price since this is the economic effect of such instruments. Most stock based compensation contracts will automatically vest in a change of control situation. Those that are in the money will need to be bought out just like shares. The treasury method is used to assess the dilutive impact of such instruments. It assumes that the proceeds from the exercise of the options (nil in the case of stock compensation units) will be used to reduce the dilutive impact of the security by buying back shares. It is an intrinsic value based method which calculates the relative value in the options. The calculation is:

$$\left(\frac{\text{Share price - strike price}}{\text{Share price}}\right) * \text{number outstanding}$$

If the options are out of the money, this calculation will give a negative result which is illogical. This is easily solved by using a MAX function which compares the above with zero:

$$\text{MAX}\left[\left(\frac{\text{Share price - strike price}}{\text{Share price}}\right) * \text{number outstanding, 0}\right]$$

The result of this calculation gives the net impact on the share count of these securities given the current share price and is added to the basic shares outstanding to give the diluted share count.

One final point, this calculation, when done for the target, uses the offer price rather than the share price.

Diluted shares outstanding...

Ensure all dilutive contracts are included. It is easy to omit items such as restricted stock units

Dilution Calculations - Buyer			
No.	Strike	Net new	
8.300	42.16	1.9	MAX((Share price - strike price) / share price * no. options,0)
10.700	0.00	10.7	MAX((Share price - strike price) / share price * no. options,0)
Net new no.		**12.6**	Sum

Dilution Calculations - Target			
No.	Strike	Net new	
54.200	27.71	17.5	MAX((Offer price - strike price) / offer price * no. options,0)
14.200	0.00	14.2	MAX((Offer price - strike price) / offer price * no. options,0)
Net new no.		**31.7**	Sum

Be careful when doing the target calculations. The strike price will be given in local currency therefore the offer price used must be in the target and not the buyer currency.

No. shares	Buyer	Target
Basic	3,257.0	1,748.1
Dilution	12.6	31.7
Diluted - DSO	3,269.6	1,779.8

Step 3 - gather historical balance sheet data

Take the data from the latest available balance sheet. Given this is a quick and dirty model, it is imperative that the line items are aggregated so that key information is easily available. This maximizes the output given the time it will take to crunch the numbers. The target information has the foreign exchange rate applied to convert the numbers into the buyer currency.

FX issues...

The target data may need to be converted into the buyer currency using an exchange rate

Balance Sheet Information			
	Buyer	**Target**	
	31 Dec XX	31 Dec XX	
Cash	16,246.0	2,320.3	Target * fx rate
PP&E	21,438.0	12,898.3	Target * fx rate
Goodwill	27,031.0	35,402.9	Target * fx rate
Other assets	46,926.0	38,492.8	Target * fx rate
Total assets	**111,641.0**	**89,114.3**	
Debt	20,100.0	26,862.7	Target * fx rate
Other liabs.	28,943.0	28,638.6	Target * fx rate
SE	62,598.0	33,613.0	Target * fx rate
Total L&E	**111,641.0**	**89,114.3**	
Check	*OK*	*OK*	

Step 4 - gather historical and forecast income statement / profit and loss data

Use key income statement / profit and loss data from latest available filings. Again, the target numbers must be adjusted by the foreign exchange rate. All line items should be normalized.

Income Statement Information - Buyer			
		Buyer	
	XX H	XY E	XZ E
Sales	87,906.0	87,463.0	92,158.0
EBITDA	17,220.0	16,328.0	17,438.0
EBIT	14,038.0	13,026.0	14,036.0
EPS - diluted	3.04	3.26	3.64

Income Statement Information - Target				
		Target - ECU		
	XX H	XY E	XZ E	
Sales	48,365.3	50,154.8	51,659.5	Target * fx rate
EBITDA	7,545.0	8,175.2	8,523.8	Target * fx rate
EBIT	5,984.9	6,584.7	6,899.6	Target * fx rate
EPS - diluted	1.84	2.11	2.28	Target * fx rate

Step 5 - calculate valuation information

Calculate both equity value (market cap) and enterprise value for both the buyer and the target. For the target, calculate both the unaffected value and the offer value by using the share price and the offer price respectively. It should be noted that the unaffected price uses diluted shares outstanding from step 2. In the dilution calculations for the target, the offer price was used which means that this unaffected value is not really unaffected. Generally this is a reasonable simplification to use since it is highly unlikely that the dilution is significant. If it is material, two dilution calculations should be done for the target, one using share price which feeds the unaffected valuation and one using offer price which feeds the offer value calculations.

Valuation	Buyer	Target	
Unaffected market cap.	179,011.1	52,448.5	Share price * DSO
Equity purchase price	nm	68,183.0	Offer price * target DSO
Net debt	3,854.0	24,542.4	Balance sheet
Unaffected enterprise value	182,865.1	76,990.9	Market cap. + net debt
Offer enterprise value	nm	92,725.4	Equity purchase price + net debt

Step 6 - make assumptions relating to the deal

Deal Assumptions		
% Stock consideration	70.0%	
% Debt and cash consideration	30.0%	1 - stock consideration
Maximum buyer cash available	10,000.0	
Fees (% of acquisition EV)	1.0%	
Buyer marginal tax rate	25.3%	
Target marginal tax rate	36.9%	
Interest on deal debt pre-tax	6.0%	
Interest on deal debt post-tax	4.5%	Pre-tax * (1 - Buyer MTR)
Interest on buyer cash pre-tax	1.0%	
Interest on buyer cash post-tax	0.7%	Pre-tax * (1 - Buyer MTR)
Annual synergies pre-tax	1,000.0	

Sources of funds...

In this case, the buyer is financing the deal with three different sources. Debt will only be issued if the stock and balance sheet cash are insufficient

Step 7 - calculate sources and uses of funds

In this case, there are two uses of funds - buying the equity and paying the deal fees. Funds need to be raised to cover this total deal cost. There are three possible sources, debt, equity and balance sheet cash, all of which are used in this example.

Sources and Uses of Funds			
Equity purchase price	68,183.0		From valuation
Advisory fees	927.3		% of EV
Total Uses of Funds	**69,110.3**		Sum
		% of total	
Buyer's cash	10,000.0	14.5%	MIN(Cash needed, cash available)
Debt issuance	11,382.2	16.5%	Total uses - cash used - stock issued
Stock issuance	47,728.1	69.1%	% Stock * equity purchase price
Total Sources of Funds	**69,110.3**	**100.0%**	Sum

Debt issuance is a plug number and will only be undertaken if the stock issuance and the balance sheet cash are insufficient to meet the total deal cost (total uses of funds). The cash number is the amount of cash needed subject to the maximum available balance sheet cash. The formula is as follows:

MIN(Total uses - stock issuance, cash available)

Taking the minimum means that if the cash needed is bigger than the cash available the model will pull the cash available number. If, on the other hand, the cash needed is smaller than the pot of balance sheet cash available then it will use the cash needed number. We can stress test this formula by thinking about an extreme financing structure. If the deal is financed 100% with stock then the only cash that is needed is the amount necessary to pay the deal fees. If we change the assumptions to 100% stock financing then the buyer's cash number in the sources of funds should equal the advisory fees in the uses of funds.

Be careful

If 100% stock is used then the buyers' cash will still be needed to pay the fees. Stress test the model to ensure working correctly for all variants of assumptions

Deal Assumptions		
% Stock consideration	100.0%	Set to 100%
% Debt and cash consideration	0.0%	1 - stock consideration
Maximum buyer cash available	10,000.0	
Fees (% of acquisition EV)	1.0%	
Buyer marginal tax rate	25.3%	
Target marginal tax rate	36.9%	
Interest on deal debt pre-tax	6.0%	
Interest on deal debt post-tax	4.5%	Pre-tax * (1 - Buyer MTR)
Interest on buyer cash pre-tax	1.0%	
Interest on buyer cash post-tax	0.7%	Pre-tax * (1 - Buyer MTR)
Annual synergies pre-tax	1,000.0	

Sources and Uses of Funds			
Equity purchase price	68,183.0		From valuation
Advisory fees	927.3		% of EV
Total Uses of Funds	**69,110.3**		Sum
		% of total	
Buyer's cash	927.3	1.3%	MIN(Cash needed, cash available)
Debt issuance	0.0	0.0%	Total uses - cash used - stock issued
Stock issuance	68,183.0	98.7%	% Stock * equity purchase price
Total Sources of Funds	**69,110.3**	**100.0%**	Sum

Step 8 - calculate consolidated DSO

If equity is being issued to do the deal then the consolidated DSO will be bigger than the current standalone DSO of the buyer. Start with the current DSO of the buyer and increase it by the number of shares that must be issued to do the deal. This is calculated by taking the money amount of equity to be issued (from the sources of funds calculation in step 7) and divide it by the buyer share price. This gives the number of shares that will be issued.

Combo Shares Calculation		
No. shares - buyer	3,269.6	From Step 2
No. new shares	871.7	Equity issued / BUY share price
No. shares - combo	**4,141.4**	Sum

Step 9 - calculate goodwill

The goodwill calculation takes the price paid for the equity and compares it with the shareholders' equity purchased. The shareholders' equity purchased is represented by the assets and liabilities of the target business so some calculations use net assets (total assets less total liabilities) while others use shareholders' equity. The fundamental accounting equation means that they are, by definition, the same number.

Total assets - total liabilities = Shareholders' equity

In theory, the net assets (or shareholders' equity) should be included at fair value but in a quick and dirty model it is easiest to assume that book amount equals fair value. This means that the values from the latest available balance sheet are used in the goodwill calculation with one exception. The value of any goodwill amount in the target balance sheet is always reduced to zero. This is because goodwill is not an "identifiable" asset since it cannot be bought or sold in its own right. This means that its value, when separately identified must be zero.

The process of reducing the target net assets by the amount of target goodwill simply makes the deal goodwill increase by the same amount. In practice, this means that the target goodwill is simply re-categorized as deal goodwill. This will be significant in any situation where goodwill amortization is calculated. This is the case, in some countries, where this goodwill is tax deductible on an amortized basis. For detailed fair value adjustments see the goodwill calculation in the fully integrated merger modeling section of this manual, step 6, page 36.

Always check...

Target existing goodwill and reduce to zero to consolidate

Goodwill Calculation		
Equity purchase price	68,183.0	Uses of funds
Target equity	33,613.0	Target balance sheet
- Existing target goodwill	(35,402.9)	Target balance sheet
= Fair value of net assets purchased	**(1,789.9)**	Sum
GOODWILL	**69,972.9**	Price paid - Net assets bought

Step 10 - consolidate the balance sheet

Consolidating any line item involves the following process:

Buyer + Target + / - Deal changes = Combo

So the trick is to understand the deal changes before doing the consolidation. All deal changes will come from one of two sources in the model and so these should be carefully reviewed before starting. The sources and uses table (step 7) and the goodwill calculations (step 9) are the "go to" areas of the model.

Don't forget...

Fees... if omitted the consolidated balance sheet will not balance by that amount

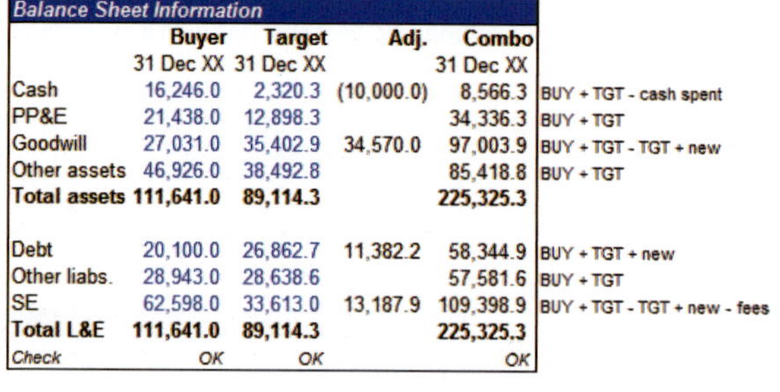

Balance Sheet Information	Buyer	Target	Adj.	Combo	
	31 Dec XX	31 Dec XX		31 Dec XX	
Cash	16,246.0	2,320.3	(10,000.0)	8,566.3	BUY + TGT - cash spent
PP&E	21,438.0	12,898.3		34,336.3	BUY + TGT
Goodwill	27,031.0	35,402.9	34,570.0	97,003.9	BUY + TGT - TGT + new
Other assets	46,926.0	38,492.8		85,418.8	BUY + TGT
Total assets	**111,641.0**	**89,114.3**		**225,325.3**	
Debt	20,100.0	26,862.7	11,382.2	58,344.9	BUY + TGT + new
Other liabs.	28,943.0	28,638.6		57,581.6	BUY + TGT
SE	62,598.0	33,613.0	13,187.9	109,398.9	BUY + TGT - TGT + new - fees
Total L&E	**111,641.0**	**89,114.3**		**225,325.3**	
Check	*OK*	*OK*		*OK*	

The deal changes in the example above - from top to bottom - are as follows:

- Cash spent on the deal is from the sources of funds
- Deal goodwill less the target goodwill reduced to zero both come from the goodwill calculation
- Debt issued is from the sources of funds
- Equity issued less target equity bought less fees are from the sources of funds, goodwill calculation and uses of funds respectively

It is vital to note that every line item in both the sources and uses and the goodwill calculation is a deal change in the consolidated balance sheet.

Top tip...

Each line item in the sources and uses and the goodwill calculations have a place in the consolidation deal changes

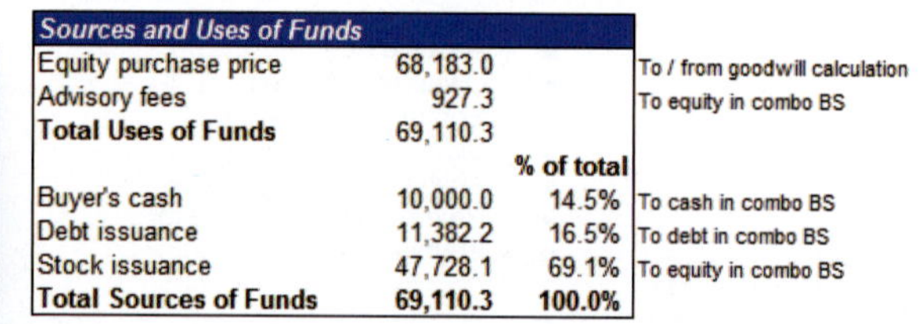

Sources and Uses of Funds			
Equity purchase price	68,183.0		To / from goodwill calculation
Advisory fees	927.3		To equity in combo BS
Total Uses of Funds	69,110.3		
		% of total	
Buyer's cash	10,000.0	14.5%	To cash in combo BS
Debt issuance	11,382.2	16.5%	To debt in combo BS
Stock issuance	47,728.1	69.1%	To equity in combo BS
Total Sources of Funds	**69,110.3**	**100.0%**	

Step 11 - consolidate the income statement / profit and loss

The consolidation logic used for the balance sheet in step 10 is the same as that used for the income statement / profit and loss.

Buyer + Target + / - Deal changes = Combo

In this case, the deal changes must be evaluated to determine if they impact the post-deal income statement / profit and loss. An equity issuance will not have any impact on the post-deal income statement / profit and loss, for example, whereas a debt issuance will result in extra interest expense. The income statement / profit and loss deal changes in this example are as follows:

- Synergies will increase EBITDA (pre-tax), EBIT(pre-tax) and NI (post-tax). The tax rate used is normally that of the target since this is typically where synergies arise
- Interest expense on deal debt (post-tax) will reduce NI
- Interest income and NI (post-tax)
- Post-tax interest income lost from cash spent on the deal will reduce NI

Combo Income Statement	XY E	XZ E	
Sales	137,617.8	143,817.5	BUY sales + TGT sales
EBITDA	24,503.2	25,961.8	BUY EBITDA + TGT EBITDA
EBIT	19,610.7	20,935.6	BUY EBIT + TGT EBIT
+ Net Income - BUY	10,658.9	11,901.4	EPS * BUY DSO
+ Net Income - TGT	3,755.5	4,058.0	EPS * TGT DSO
+ Synergies post-tax	631.0	631.0	Assumption * (1 - MTR)
- Interest on new debt post-tax	(510.1)	(510.1)	Debt issued * post-tax cost
- Interest on cash spent post-tax	(74.7)	(74.7)	Cash spent * post-tax rate
= Combo net income	14,460.5	16,005.6	BUY NI + TGT NI + / deal changes
Combo EPS	3.49	3.86	Combo NI / Combo DSO

Merger consequences analysis

Further critical analysis is possible from this slightly more detailed merger model including:

- EPS accretion / dilution
- Synergies to breakeven
- Relative PEs
- Ownership dilution
- Contribution analysis
- Side by side comparison
- Analysis at various prices
- Return on invested capital
- Premium analysis

Merger consequences analysis - EPS accretion / dilution

EPS accretion / dilution is widely used in deal analysis. It shows the extent to which EPS will increase or decrease as a result of the deal.

Naturally, it is purely earnings focused, and ignores key items such as the cost of any equity issued. Its narrow focus means that EPS accretion / dilution should not be used in isolation. A deal that is EPS accretive may not necessarily be a good deal.

Finally, if your analysis suggests that the deal is highly accretive, as is the case here, then it is important to ask if there are some other reasons why such a deal has not been done or attempted already. There might be issues associated with competition authorities or some such which makes a deal less attractive to a buyer.

EPS accretion / dilution	XY E	XZ E	
Combo EPS	3.49	3.86	Combo NI / Combo DSO
Buyer EPS	3.26	3.64	From Step 2
Accretion (Dilution) %	**7.1%**	**6.2%**	(Combo EPS / BUY EPS) -1
Synergies to breakeven	0.0	0.0	(BUY EPS - Combo EPS) * combo DSO / (1 - MTR)

In the case above, there are only two years of analysis where a small dilution is seen in both years. A longer EPS profile would be helpful.

Merger consequences analysis - synergies to breakeven

This calculates the additional synergies needed to achieve zero EPS accretion / dilution. In this case, they are zero (see above) because the deal is already accretive using the assumptions given.

Building this calculation up in stages, the first stage is to calculate the EPS needed to achieve breakeven. This is:

Buyer standalone EPS - Consolidated EPS

However, it is unusual in the context of a deal to reference synergies on a per share basis so the next stage grosses this up as follows:

(Buyer standalone EPS - Consolidated EPS) * Consolidated DSO

This gives a gross number, based on net income, which is a post-tax number but it is more common to reference pre-tax numbers for synergies so it must be grossed up for tax:

$$\frac{\text{(Buyer standalone EPS - Consolidated EPS) * Consolidate DSO}}{\text{(1 - MTR)}}$$

Finally, if the deal is accretive already then the answer to this calculation is zero. The formula above will give a negative result which is mathematically correct but does not make sense. An easy fix is to wrap this formula within a MAX function which compares it to zero. The final version becomes:

$$\text{MAX}\left[\frac{\text{(Buyer standalone EPS - Consolidated EPS) * Consolidate DSO}}{\text{(1 - MTR)}}, 0\right]$$

This can be stress tested by changing assumptions so that the deal is dilutive, in this case, change the deal so it is 100% stock financed. This means no debt or balance sheet cash is being used. Setting the synergy assumption to zero also means this calculation will give the total (rather than additional) synergies to breakeven.

Breakeven synergies...

It is useful to sanity check how achievable synergies are by using comparable transaction data

Deal Assumptions		
% Stock consideration	100.0%	Set to 100%
% Debt and cash consideration	0.0%	1 - stock consideration
Maximum buyer cash available	0.0	Set to zero
Fees (% of acquisition EV)	1.0%	
Buyer marginal tax rate	25.3%	
Target marginal tax rate	36.9%	
Interest on deal debt pre-tax	6.0%	
Interest on deal debt post-tax	4.5%	Pre-tax * (1 - Buyer MTR)
Interest on buyer cash pre-tax	1.0%	
Interest on buyer cash post-tax	0.7%	Pre-tax * (1 - Buyer MTR)
Annual synergies pre-tax	0.0	Set to zero

EPS accretion / dilution	XY E	XZ E	
Combo EPS	3.18	3.53	Combo NI / Combo DSO
Buyer EPS	3.26	3.64	From Step 2
Accretion (Dilution) %	**(2.4%)**	**(3.1%)**	(Combo EPS / BUY EPS) -1
Synergies to breakeven	548.3	818.7	(BUY EPS - Combo EPS) * combo DSO / (1 - MTR)

Next, copy and paste this value into the synergy assumption and the EPS accretion / dilution will be zero. If it is not, then the integrity of the model is questionable and needs to be checked in detail to identify the source of the error.

Deal Assumptions		
% Stock consideration	100.0%	Set to 100%
% Debt and cash consideration	0.0%	1 - stock consideration
Maximum buyer cash available	0.0	Set to zero
Fees (% of acquisition EV)	1.0%	
Buyer marginal tax rate	25.3%	
Target marginal tax rate	36.9%	
Interest on deal debt pre-tax	6.0%	
Interest on deal debt post-tax	4.5%	Pre-tax * (1 - Buyer MTR)
Interest on buyer cash pre-tax	1.0%	
Interest on buyer cash post-tax	0.7%	Pre-tax * (1 - Buyer MTR)
Annual synergies pre-tax	548.3	Copy and paste value

EPS accretion / dilution	XY E	XZ E	
Combo EPS	3.26	3.60	Combo NI / Combo DSO
Buyer EPS	3.26	3.64	From Step 2
Accretion (Dilution) %	**0.0%**	**(1.0%)**	(Combo EPS / BUY EPS) -1
Synergies to breakeven	0.0	270.5	(BUY EPS - Combo EPS) * combo DSO / (1 - MTR)

Merger consequences analysis - relative PEs

Deal Analysis	*XY E*	*XZ E*	
Buyer P/E	16.8 x	15.0 x	BUY share price / BUY EPS
Offer P/E	18.2 x	16.8 x	Offer price / TGT EPS
Debt P/E	22.3 x	22.3 x	1 / post-tax cost of debt
Cash P/E	133.9 x	133.9 x	1 / post-tax interest rate

A comparison of the buyer PE and the offer (acquisition) PE gives you a quick analysis of the deal. In the simplest situation of a 100% stock or a 100% cash deal with zero synergies, it will give you the same answer as EPS accretion / dilution. Consequently it should always be used as a stress test of the model, at the very least.

The offer (or acquisition) PE gives an indication of the implied return on equity from this investment. It compares the prices being paid with the earnings being bought. If you calculate the inverse you will get the answer in % terms rather than multiple terms. In this example, the year 1 offer PE is 18.2 x which implies a 5.5% return on equity.

The return on equity should be compared to the cost of equity to establish whether or not it is sufficient. If the financing is all stock the implied cost equity is provided by the buyer PE. This gives us the market demand in earnings for every $ invested. Again, the inverse of the PE gives this data in percentage terms. In this case, the buyer PE in the first year is 16.8 x which implies a cost of stock financing of 6.0%.

An investment expected to yield 5.5% and financed with financing costing 6.0% is not, on the face of it, a good deal. This is easily seen by comparing the PEs. The buyer PE is lower than the offer PE, which means that the cost of raising buyer equity is higher than return expected from the target equity being purchased. The buyer PE needs to be higher than the offer PE in order for the deal to be accretive. Since this analysis only uses the standalone numbers then incremental changes, such as synergies, are not taken into account.

If the assumptions are changed to 100% stock financing and zero synergies, the relative PEs and the EPS accretion / dilution give consistent results.

PE analysis...

If financing is all stock or all debt and synergies are zero then the PE analysis and the EPS accretion/ dilution will be consistent... if not... check your model to establish why not

Deal Assumptions		
% Stock consideration	100.0%	Set to 100%
% Debt and cash consideration	0.0%	1 - stock consideration
Maximum buyer cash available	0.0	Set to zero
Fees (% of acquisition EV)	1.0%	
Buyer marginal tax rate	25.3%	
Target marginal tax rate	36.9%	
Interest on deal debt pre-tax	6.0%	
Interest on deal debt post-tax	4.5%	Pre-tax * (1 - Buyer MTR)
Interest on buyer cash pre-tax	1.0%	
Interest on buyer cash post-tax	0.7%	Pre-tax * (1 - Buyer MTR)
Annual synergies pre-tax	0.0	Set to zero

EPS accretion / dilution	XY E	XZ E	
Combo EPS	3.18	3.53	Combo NI / Combo DSO
Buyer EPS	3.26	3.64	From Step 2
Accretion (Dilution) %	**(2.4%)**	**(3.1%)**	(Combo EPS / BUY EPS) -1
Synergies to breakeven	548.3	818.7	(BUY EPS - Combo EPS) * combo DSO / (1 - MTR)

Deal Analysis	*XY E*	*XZ E*	
Buyer P/E	16.8 x	15.0 x	BUY share price / BUY EPS
Offer P/E	18.2 x	16.8 x	Offer price / TGT EPS
Debt P/E	22.3 x	22.3 x	1 / post-tax cost of debt
Cash P/E	133.9 x	133.9 x	1 / post-tax interest rate

But what if the financing were different? If cash is paid by issuing debt then the cost of financing is the post-tax cost of debt, in this case, 4.5%. This means that if the implied return on equity purchased is 5.5% and it is financed with debt costing 4.5%, it seems to be a viable deal. Running the numbers with 100% debt financing and zero synergies, this is exactly what is seen - an accretive deal.

Deal Assumptions		
% Stock consideration	0.0%	Set to zero
% Debt and cash consideration	100.0%	1 - stock consideration
Maximum buyer cash available	0.0	Set to zero
Fees (% of acquisition EV)	1.0%	
Buyer marginal tax rate	25.3%	
Target marginal tax rate	36.9%	
Interest on deal debt pre-tax	6.0%	
Interest on deal debt post-tax	4.5%	Pre-tax * (1 - Buyer MTR)
Interest on buyer cash pre-tax	1.0%	
Interest on buyer cash post-tax	0.7%	Pre-tax * (1 - Buyer MTR)
Annual synergies pre-tax	0.0	Set to zero

EPS accretion / dilution	XY E	XZ E	
Combo EPS	3.46	3.93	Combo NI / Combo DSO
Buyer EPS	3.26	3.64	From Step 2
Accretion (Dilution) %	**6.2%**	**8.1%**	(Combo EPS / BUY EPS) -1
Synergies to breakeven	0.0	0.0	(BUY EPS - Combo EPS) * combo DSO / (1 - MTR)

Deal Analysis	XY E	XZ E	
Buyer P/E	16.8 x	15.0 x	BUY share price / BUY EPS
Offer P/E	18.2 x	16.8 x	Offer price / TGT EPS
Debt P/E	22.3 x	22.3 x	1 / post-tax cost of debt
Cash P/E	133.9 x	133.9 x	1 / post-tax interest rate

If the deal were financed entirely with balance sheet cash it is likely (all other things being equal) to be even more accretive since the post-tax interest income lost (cost of finance) is 0.7% with an expected return on the equity bought of 5.5%.

It is more common, in the industry, to do this analysis using PEs rather than percentages. To calculate the "debt PE", simply take the inverse of the post-tax cost of debt. In this case this gives a multiple of 22.3 x and similarly with the "Cash PE" where the inverse of the post-tax lost interest income gives a multiple of 133.9 x.

The PE of the financing must be higher than the offer PE in order to produce an accretive deal. In this case, the offer PE is higher than the buyer PE but lower than the debt and cash PEs which implies dilution if 100% stock financing is used but accretion if 100% debt / cash is used. When the model is stress tested using these assumptions and zero synergies this is, in fact, what is observed for EPS accretion / dilution. These stress tests should always be done in order to check the model is working as expected.

One final point, this check works very well at the financing extremes (100% stock or 100% debt) but does not predict well when a mix of financing is used. This is the reason why stress testing by changing the assumptions is critical to test the integrity of the model.

In summary:

If the buyer PE > offer PE the deal is likely to be accretive
If the buyer PE < offer PE the deal is likely to be dilutive
If the debt or cash PE > offer PE the deal is likely to be accretive
If the debt or cash PE < offer PE the deal is likely to be dilutive

A comparison of the buyer PE and the offer PE gives you a quick and dirty view of the deal. In the simplest situation of 100% stock or 100% cash deal with zero synergies, it will give you the same answer as EPS accretion / dilution. Consequently it should always be used as a stress test of the model, at the very least.

Merger consequences analysis - ownership dilution

This is important when some or all of the consideration is with stock. It shows the extent to which the buyer shareholders are "giving away" their ownership in the business to pay for the deal. The calculation is straightforward:

$$\frac{\text{Buyer DSO standalone}}{\text{Consolidate DSO}}$$

This shows the percentage ownership in the post-deal world. A key question for the deal team is to understand whether this will be acceptable to the buying shareholders.

Finally, this means we can calculate the exchange ratio. This is the number of buyer shares that a target shareholder will receive in exchange for shares in the target company.

$$\frac{\text{Buyer shares issued (from consolidated DSO calculation}}{\text{Target shares purchased}}$$

Or:

$$\frac{\text{Offer price}}{\text{Buyer share price}} * \text{\% stock financing}$$

It is generally shown to four or five decimal places and is always communicated to the target shareholders in the offer document. In this case the selling shareholders will receive 0.48979 buyer shares and 11.49 (offer price * debt / cash assumption) in cash for every share sold.

This can be checked easily as follows:

Offer price...

The cash per share and the exchange ratio is communicated to the selling shareholders in the offer document

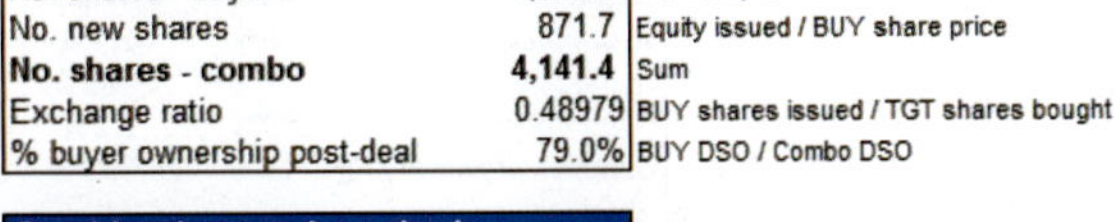

Combo Shares Calculation		
No. shares - buyer	3,269.6	From Step 2
No. new shares	871.7	Equity issued / BUY share price
No. shares - combo	**4,141.4**	Sum
Exchange ratio	0.48979	BUY shares issued / TGT shares bought
% buyer ownership post-deal	79.0%	BUY DSO / Combo DSO

Consideration per share check		
Offer price per share	**38.31**	From Step 1
Stock value per share	26.82	Exchange ratio * BUY share price
Cash per share	11.49	Offer price * % cash consideraton
Total value per share	**38.31**	Sum stock + cash value

So in this deal, the buyer has agreed to deliver 38.31 per share to the buyer and the current assumptions mean that this will be done by providing buyer shares worth 26.82 with 11.49 in cash.

Merger consequences analysis - contribution analysis

This takes key income statement / profit and loss metrics and calculates the proportion of the consolidated numbers going forward being provided or contributed by each of the parties. This can be compared with the % ownership of the combined entity and gives a view of the reasonableness of the offer compared to both parties contribution to the combined entity. It is particularly useful in an all stock deal.

Contribution Analysis

	Sales			
	XX H	XY E	XZ E	
Buyer	87,906.0	87,463.0	92,158.0	BUY sales
% contribution	*64.5%*	*63.6%*	*64.1%*	BUY / proforma
Target	48,365.3	50,154.8	51,659.5	TGT sales
% contribution	*35.5%*	*36.4%*	*35.9%*	TGT / proforma
Synergies	0.0	0.0	0.0	Assumption
% contribution	*0.0%*	*0.0%*	*0.0%*	Assumption / proforma
Combo / proforma	136,271.3	137,617.8	143,817.5	BUY + TGT + synergies

Sales

XZ E
XY E
XX H
0% 20% 40% 60% 80% 100%
Buyer Target

From the sales analysis above, it can be seen, that in each of the years examined, the buyer provided approximately 64% of the revenues with the remaining 36% coming from the target.

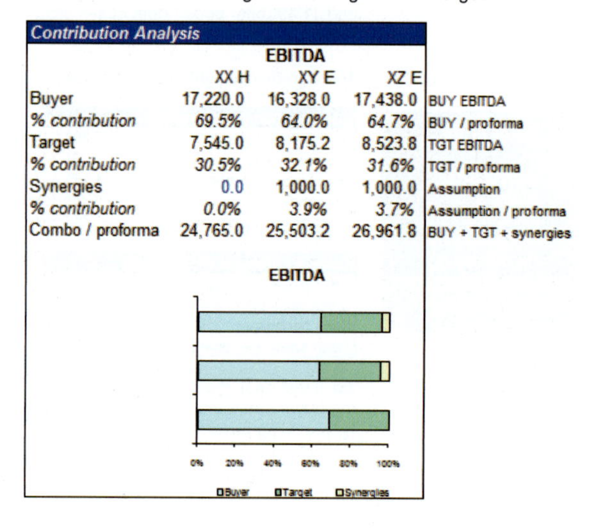

Contribution Analysis

	EBITDA			
	XX H	XY E	XZ E	
Buyer	17,220.0	16,328.0	17,438.0	BUY EBITDA
% contribution	*69.5%*	*64.0%*	*64.7%*	BUY / proforma
Target	7,545.0	8,175.2	8,523.8	TGT EBITDA
% contribution	*30.5%*	*32.1%*	*31.6%*	TGT / proforma
Synergies	0.0	1,000.0	1,000.0	Assumption
% contribution	*0.0%*	*3.9%*	*3.7%*	Assumption / proforma
Combo / proforma	24,765.0	25,503.2	26,961.8	BUY + TGT + synergies

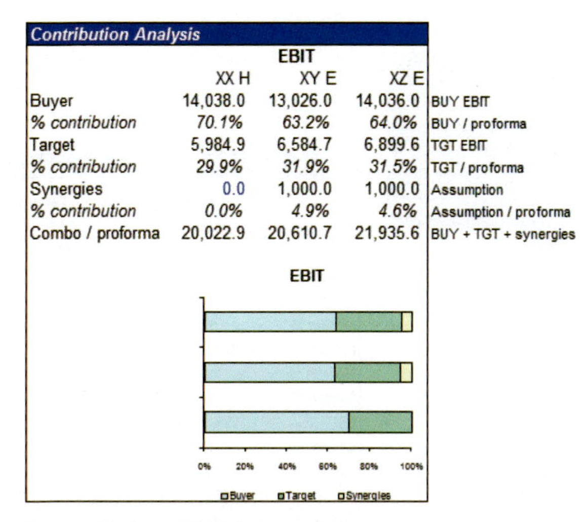

Contribution Analysis

	EBIT			
	XX H	XY E	XZ E	
Buyer	14,038.0	13,026.0	14,036.0	BUY EBIT
% contribution	*70.1%*	*63.2%*	*64.0%*	BUY / proforma
Target	5,984.9	6,584.7	6,899.6	TGT EBIT
% contribution	*29.9%*	*31.9%*	*31.5%*	TGT / proforma
Synergies	0.0	1,000.0	1,000.0	Assumption
% contribution	*0.0%*	*4.9%*	*4.6%*	Assumption / proforma
Combo / proforma	20,022.9	20,610.7	21,935.6	BUY + TGT + synergies

For both EBIT and EBITDA above, the buyer is expected to provide around 64% of the profits with 31% coming from the target and the remaining 5% from the synergies.

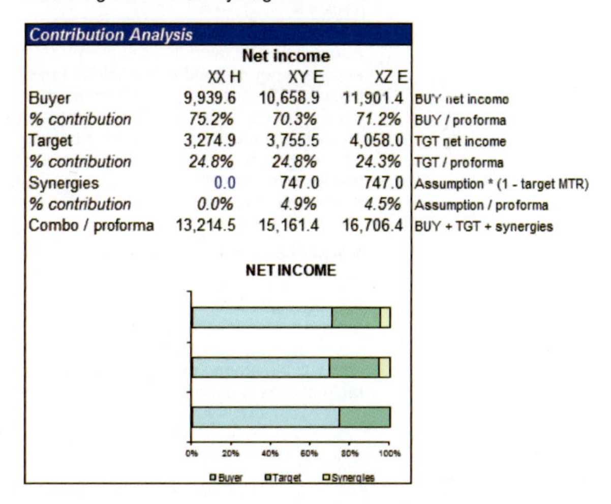

Contribution Analysis

	Net income			
	XX H	XY E	XZ E	
Buyer	9,939.6	10,658.9	11,901.4	BUY net income
% contribution	*75.2%*	*70.3%*	*71.2%*	BUY / proforma
Target	3,274.9	3,755.5	4,058.0	TGT net income
% contribution	*24.8%*	*24.8%*	*24.3%*	TGT / proforma
Synergies	0.0	747.0	747.0	Assumption * (1 - target MTR)
% contribution	*0.0%*	*4.9%*	*4.5%*	Assumption / proforma
Combo / proforma	13,214.5	15,161.4	16,706.4	BUY + TGT + synergies

At the net income level, the buyer is expected to contribute 71% of the profits with 24% coming from the target with the remaining 5% coming from the synergies.

Look-up...

This table of data is invaluable as a quick reference for the impact of valuation changes

Merger consequences analysis - side by side comparison

This analysis lines up the key income statement / profit and loss performance indicators for both parties. It is incredibly useful when putting together a proposal that makes sense or for analyzing the relative strengths or weaknesses of a proposed deal structure.

Side-by-Side Comparison

	Buyer		Target		Combo	
	XY E	XZ E	XY E	XZ E	XY E	XZ E
Sales	87,463.0	92,158.0	50,154.8	51,659.5	137,617.8	143,817.5
Growth %	*nm*	*5.4%*	*nm*	*3.0%*	*nm*	*4.5%*
Synergies	0.0	0.0	0.0	0.0	1,000.0	1,000.0
Margin %	*nm*	*nm*	*nm*	*nm*	*0.7%*	*0.7%*
EBITDA	16,328.0	17,438.0	8,175.2	8,523.8	25,503.2	26,961.8
Growth %	*nm*	*6.8%*	*nm*	*4.3%*	*nm*	*5.7%*
Margin %	*18.7%*	*18.9%*	*16.3%*	*16.5%*	*18.5%*	*18.7%*
EBIT	13,026.0	14,036.0	6,584.7	6,899.6	20,610.7	21,935.6
Growth %	*nm*	*7.8%*	*nm*	*4.8%*	*nm*	*6.4%*
Margin %	*14.9%*	*15.2%*	*13.1%*	*13.4%*	*15.0%*	*15.3%*
Net income	10,658.9	11,901.4	3,755.5	4,058.0	14,460.5	16,005.6
Growth %	*nm*	*11.7%*	*nm*	*8.1%*	*nm*	*10.7%*
Margin %	*12.2%*	*12.9%*	*7.5%*	*7.9%*	*10.5%*	*11.1%*
EPS	3.26	3.64	2.11	2.28	3.49	3.86
Growth %	*nm*	*11.7%*	*nm*	*8.1%*	*nm*	*10.7%*

Above it can be seen that the growth rates shown by the combined entity are not as good as that of the buyer standalone. This is because the target is showing lower growth expectations. The margins of the buyer are also better than the target but this is flowing through to the combined numbers because of the expectations regarding synergies. An assessment of the risk of achievement of these synergies will need to be undertaken since the target will drag down the buyer's margins if they are not realized.

Merger consequences analysis - analysis at various prices

This is a key look up table for use throughout the deal analysis. Any conversations will often revolve around offer price and this table summarizes the valuation impact of differing offer prices. Consequently, it should be immediately referred to when having discussions around pricing. As with all comparables, the value of this table of data is dependent on the use of appropriate benchmarks.

Analysis at Various Prices									
Offer	Offer	Equity	Offer	EV/EBITDA			P/E		
Price	Prem.	Value	EV	XX H	XY E	XZ E	XX H	XY E	XZ E
29.47	0%	52,448	76,991	10.2 x	9.4 x	9.0 x	16.0 x	14.0 x	12.9 x
32.41	10%	57,693	82,236	10.9 x	10.1 x	9.6 x	17.6 x	15.4 x	14.2 x
35.36	20%	62,938	87,481	11.6 x	10.7 x	10.3 x	19.2 x	16.8 x	15.5 x
38.31	30%	68,183	92,725	12.3 x	11.3 x	10.9 x	20.8 x	18.2 x	16.8 x
41.26	40%	73,428	97,970	13.0 x	12.0 x	11.5 x	22.4 x	19.6 x	18.1 x
44.20	50%	78,673	103,215	13.7 x	12.6 x	12.1 x	24.0 x	20.9 x	19.4 x
47.15	60%	83,918	108,460	14.4 x	13.3 x	12.7 x	25.6 x	22.3 x	20.7 x
50.10	70%	89,162	113,705	15.1 x	13.9 x	13.3 x	27.2 x	23.7 x	22.0 x
53.04	80%	94,407	118,950	15.8 x	14.6 x	14.0 x	28.8 x	25.1 x	23.3 x
55.99	90%	99,652	124,194	16.5 x	15.2 x	14.6 x	30.4 x	26.5 x	24.6 x
58.94	100%	104,897	129,439	17.2 x	15.8 x	15.2 x	32.0 x	27.9 x	25.8 x
Trading comps - median				10.1 x	9.5 x	8.8 x	15.8 x	14.4 x	13.1 x
Transaction comps - median				14.1 x	na	na	na	na	na
Buyer				10.6 x	11.2 x	10.5 x	18.0 x	16.8 x	15.0 x

Merger consequences analysis - return on invested capital

This is a quick and dirty calculation which compares the cost of the target with the incremental profits it delivers. The calculation must start with the definition of invested capital. It is the offer enterprise value plus the fees associated with the transaction. This gives the total investment in the acquisition of the target business.

The next step is to calculate the profit generated by the target. Here it is incremental profits to the buyer that needs to be considered. In principle, this is the profit provided by the target plus the synergies that are expected as a result of doing the deal. These synergies are incremental to the deal and should be included in the analysis.

Given invested capital is enterprise value then the level of profit to be analyzed is EBIT after taxes - often referred to as net operating profit after taxes or NOPAT.

Return on Invested Capital	XX H	XY E	
Invested capital calculation			
Offer EV	92,725.4		From Step 5
Transaction costs	927.3		Fees
Invested capital at deal date	**93,652.7**		Offer EV + fees
Net operating profit after-tax			
Target EBIT		6,584.7	Forecast
Target effective tax rate		31.5%	Forecast
Target NOPAT		4,510.5	EBIT * (1- ETR)
Synergies pre-tax		1,000.0	Assumption
Target marginal tax rate		36.9%	Assumption
Synergies post-tax		631.0	Assumption * (1 - TGT MTR)
Target NOPAT plus synergies		**5,141.5**	TGT + post-tax synergies
Return on invested capital		**5.5%**	(TGT NOPAT plus synergies) / inv. cap.

It should be noted that the tax rate to apply to the EBIT of the target is the expected effective tax rate (ETR) of the target. ETR must be used when taxing profits. If ETR and marginal tax rate (MTR) are approximately the same then practitioners often use MTR as a shortcut. In this case there is a significant difference between ETR and MTR and therefore it is material which tax rate is used in which calculation. When taxing synergies, then MTR should be used since it is a marginal adjustment. Since the synergies are normally realized in the target then target MTR is typically used, however the MTR should really follow the location of the synergy generation.

The return is calculated as follows:

$$\frac{\text{Incremental NOPAT}}{\text{Offer EV plus fees}}$$

Merger consequences analysis - premium analysis

This analysis focuses on the premium paid for the target and compares it to the expected benefit. Calculating the premium paid is relatively straightforward by comparing the unaffected market capitalization with the offer equity price.

Next the synergy calculation must be done. This is done on a post-tax basis, since the benefit is received post-tax. Also, once the run rate of synergies is achieved they will produce an annual benefit. This means that there is a disconnect being the premium being paid now with the benefit of the synergies which is realized annually into the future. This is solved by discounting the synergies which of course leads to the final issue for this calculation - what discount rate should be used?

A fundamental principle of discounting is that the discount rate must match the risk of the cash flows being discounted. This means that if the synergies are being realized at the target then it is the target risk that must be considered. Synergies are always discussed at an operational level meaning that the discount rate must take into account the return required from all providers of capital (both debt and equity). The weighted average cost of capital (normally the target) should be used. However, most would agree that there are special risk factors applied to the realization of synergies so that frequently a “risk factor” is added to the target WACC in recognition that these particular cash flows are more risky than the average cash flows of the target. Of course, it is impossible to calculate exactly what this “risk factor” should be. A sensitivity analysis should be undertaken to establish the impact of this assumption to the analysis.

It is also reasonable to mid-year adjust the valuation since the process of discounting assumes an “end of period” timing. This is very conservative since the synergies are actually being realized over the entire course of each year. A reasonable compromise is to assume that they are realized at the mid-point of the period.

Offer Premium Analysis	XX H	XY E	
Target unaffected market cap	52,448.5		From Step 5
Target equity purchase price	68,183.0		From Step 5
Total premium paid	**15,734.5**		Difference
WACC	6.2%		Target WACC
Risk premium	3.0%		Estimate
Discount rate	9.2%		Sum
Pre-tax synergies		1,000.0	Assumption
Target marginal tax rate		36.9%	Assumption
Post-tax synergies		631.0	Assumption * (1 - TGT MTR)
Present value of synergies	6,888.6		Post - tax synergies / discount rate
Mid-year adjusted PV of synergies	**7,197.2**		PV * (1 + discount rate) ^ 0.5
Less premium paid	(15,734.5)		From above
Value created / (destroyed)	**(8,537.3)**		PV of synergies - premium

In this example, the present value of the synergies is a lot less than the premium being paid. It is important, when advising on a deal, that information, such as this, is considered, understood and evaluated.

Fully integrated three statement merger model

Introduction

Building a fully integrated three statement merger model is a time consuming process and consequently is not normally undertaken unless a very detailed analysis is required. A fully integrated three statement forecast model must first be built for both the buyer and the target respectively. The consolidation and analysis is then undertaken given the deal assumptions. The benefit of going to this level of detail is a multi-year picture of the numbers, combined with more significant capability on affordability analysis and financing structure.

Information required

- Share prices
- Basic shares outstanding
- Options information for buyer and target
- Foreign exchange rate for cross border deals
- Fully integrated three statement forecast model for the buyer
- Fully integrated three statement forecast model for the target

Assumptions needed

- Premium paid
- % stock / debt consideration
- Balance sheet cash available
- Synergies - including development over time to run rate
- Cost of debt
- Repayment schedule for deal debt - If any
- Refinancing of target debt - if any
- Rate of interest income on balance sheet cash
- Advisory fees
- Equity issuance fees
- Debt issuance fees
- Depreciation / amortization period for debt issuance fees
- Asset step-up assumptions
- Amortization life for step-ups
- Dividend assumptions for post-deal business

Analysis possible

- EPS accretion / dilution
- Synergies to breakeven
- Relative PEs
- Ownership dilution
- Contribution analysis
- Side by side comparison
- Analysis at various prices
- Return on invested capital - development over time
- Premium analysis - development over time
- Credit analysis - including affordability of new financing structure

Modeling steps

The following are the steps for a fully integrated three statement merger model. Each is dealt with in turn below.

1. Gather market data and calculate share prices
2. Calculate diluted shares outstanding (DSO)
3. Calculate valuation information
4. Make assumptions relating to the deal
5. Calculate sources and uses of funds
6. Calculate goodwill
7. Forecast any asset step-ups going forward
8. Forecast the tax impact of any asset step-ups going forward
9. Forecast deal debt going forward
10. Forecast amortization of deal debt fees going forward
11. Calculate consolidated DSO
12. Consolidate the proforma balance sheet
13. Build the consolidated income statement / profit and loss except for interest and tax expense
14. Build the consolidated balance sheet except for cash plug items
15. Build the consolidated cash flow statement
16. Plug the cash numbers from the cash flow statement into the balance sheet
17. Calculate consolidated interest
18. Calculate consolidated tax expense
19. Include interest and tax expense in the income statement / profit and loss and deal with the circular references

Step 1 - gather market data and calculate share prices

In this example, shown below, the deal is cross border. The simplest way to resolve this is to use a single foreign exchange rate and translate all the relevant target numbers using this rate. This restates the target financials to the currency of the buyer without creating any issues with foreign exchange gains and losses. A further simplification is to assume that the deal date is consistent with the latest financial year end. (See section called *Deal date different to year end* page 71).

Offer premium

Use comparable transactions data to decide what is reasonable

Market Data			
Company name	Buyer	Target	
Latest historical year end	31 Dec XX	31 Dec XX	
Currency	ECU	NVR	
Transaction date	31 Dec XX		
FX rate	0.9352		
Ticker	BUY	TGT	
Unaffected share price - NVR	nm	31.51	
Unaffected share price - ECU	54.75	29.47	Share price * fx rate
Offer premium	nm	30.0%	
Offer share price - NVR	nm	40.96	Share price * (1 + premium)
Offer share price - ECU	nm	38.31	Offer price * fx rate

Step 2 - calculate diluted shares outstanding (DSO)

This step calculates the number of diluted shares outstanding for both the buyer and target. Stock based compensation is the most common item to include in these calculations. Most of this is represented by stock options but increasingly other share based compensation, such as restricted stock units, should be included. Restricted stock units are treated as if they were options with a zero strike price since this is the economic effect of such instruments. Most stock based compensation contracts will automatically vest in a change of control situation. Those that are in the money will need to be bought out just like shares. The treasury method is used to assess the dilutive impact of such instruments. It assumes that the proceeds from the exercise of the options (nil in the case of stock compensation units) will be used to reduce the dilutive impact of the security by buying back shares. It is an intrinsic value based method which calculates the relative value in the options. The calculation is:

$$\left(\frac{\text{Share price - strike price}}{\text{Share price}}\right) \text{* number outstanding}$$

If the options are out of the money, this calculation will give a negative result which is illogical. This is easily solved by using a MAX function which compares the above with zero:

$$\text{MAX}\left[\left(\frac{\text{Share price - strike price}}{\text{Share price}}\right) \text{* number outstanding, 0}\right]$$

The result of this calculation gives the net impact on the share count of these securities given the current share price and is added to the basic shares outstanding to give the diluted share count.

One final point, this calculation, when done for the target, use the offer price rather than the share price.

Diluted shares outstanding...

Ensure all dilutive contracts are included. It is easy to omit items such as restricted stock units

Dilution Calculations - Buyer			
Number	Strike	Net new	
8.3	42.2	1.9	MAX((Share price - strike price) / share price * no. options,0)
10.7	0.0	10.7	MAX((Share price - strike price) / share price * no. options,0)
Net new no.		**12.6**	Sum

Dilution Calculations - Target			
Number	Strike	Net new	
54.2	27.7	17.5	MAX((Offer price - strike price) / offer price * no. options,0)
14.2	0.0	14.2	MAX((Offer price - strike price) / offer price * no. options,0)
Net new no.		**31.7**	Sum

Be careful when doing the target calculations. The strike price will be given in local currency therefore the offer price used must be in the target and not the buyer currency.

No. shares	Buyer	Target	
Basic	3,257.0	1,748.1	
Dilution	12.6	31.7	From dilution calculation
Diluted - DSO	**3,269.6**	**1,779.8**	Sum

Step 3 - calculate valuation information

Calculate both equity value (market cap) and enterprise value for both the buyer and the target. For the target, calculate both the unaffected value and the offer value by using the share price and the offer price respectively. It should be noted that the unaffected price uses diluted shares outstanding from step 2. In the dilution calculations for the target, the offer price was used which means that this unaffected value is not really unaffected. Generally this is a reasonable simplification to use since it is highly unlikely that the dilution is significant. If it is material, two dilution calculations should be done for the target, one using share price which feeds the unaffected valuation and one using offer price which feeds the offer value calculations.

Valuation	Buyer	Target	
Unaffected market capitalization	179,010.7	52,448.9	Share price * DSO
Equity purchase price	nm	68,183.5	Offer price * target DSO
Net debt	3,854.0	24,542.5	Balance sheet
Unaffected enterprise value	182,864.7	76,991.3	Market cap. + net debt
Offer enterprise value	nm	92,726.0	Equity purchase price + net debt

Step 4 - make assumptions relating to the deal

In this model, a number of additional assumptions are needed to model in more detail.

- A refinancing switch (1 = refinance, 0 = do not refinance) will be used in order to easily change the assumptions about refinancing of debt
- Fee assumptions are broken down into the component parts
- Asset step-up assumptions are made so that the goodwill calculation can allocate the consideration more effectively

Key Assumptions		
Interest rate on acquisition debt	6.0%	
Refinance target net debt?	1	Refinancing switch
Advisory fees, % of enterprise value	0.5%	
Debt fees, % debt issued	2.0%	
Debt fees amortization years	7.0	
Equity fees, % equity issued	2.0%	
% Stock financing	75.0%	
% Debt and cash financing	25.0%	1 - stock consideration
Maximum existing buyer cash used	10,000.0	
New intangibles valuation	4,000.0	
Amortization period (years)	20.0	
PP&E step-up amount	500.0	
Depreciation period (years)	10.0	

Step 5 - calculate sources and uses of funds

In this case there are five uses of funds, three of which are fees. The equity price comes directly from step 3. The debt refinancing takes the debt from the valuation in step 3 and multiplies it by the switch from the key assumptions block. If the switch cell shows 1, then the uses of funds will return the value to be refinanced. If, on the other hand, this cell shows 0, the uses of funds will return a zero for debt refinancing.

Sources of funds...

Watch out. In this case, the debt fees are circular. This can be avoided by a thoughtful approach to the formula build

Sources and Uses of Funds		
Equity price	68,183.5	From valuation
Debt refinancing	24,542.5	Net debt from valuation * refinancing switch
Advisory fees	463.6	% of EV
Debt issue fees	675.0	% of debt issued
Equity issue fees	1,022.8	% of stock issued
Uses of funds	**94,887.3**	Sum
Buyer's cash	10,000.0	MIN(Cash needed, cash available)
Debt issuance	33,749.7	(Uses except debt fees - cash - stock issue) / (1 - debt fee %)
Stock issuance	51,137.6	% Stock * equity purchase price
Sources of funds	**94,887.3**	Sum

Debt issuance is a plug number and will only be undertaken if the stock issuance and the balance sheet cash are insufficient to meet the total deal cost (total uses of funds). Unfortunately this will lead to a circular reference since the total uses influences the debt issued and the debt issued influences the debt fees which in turn influence the total uses. This can easily be avoided by recognizing that if the fees are 2.0% then the rest of the debt to be issued is 98.0%. So the debt issuance calculation becomes:

$$\frac{\text{Total uses except debt fees - cash used - stock issuance}}{\text{1 - debt fee \% assumption}}$$

It is very important that the "Total uses except debt fees" is calculated by summing the individual components. If total uses - debt fees is used, the circularity will not be avoided. The cash number is the amount of cash needed subject to the maximum available balance sheet cash. The formula is as follows:

MIN (Total uses except debt fees - stock issuance, cash available)

Taking the minimum means that if the cash needed is bigger than the cash available the model will pull the cash available number. If, on the other hand, the cash needed is smaller than the pot of balance sheet cash available then it will use the cash needed number. We can stress test this formula by thinking about an extreme financing structure. If the deal is financed 100% with stock and the refinancing is set to zero also, then the only cash that is needed is the amount necessary to pay the deal fees. If we change the assumptions to 100% stock financing then the buyer's cash number in the sources of funds should equal the advisory and equity issuance fees in the uses of funds.

Be careful

If 100% stock is used then the buyers' cash will still be needed to pay the fees. Stress test the model to ensure working correctly for all variants of assumptions

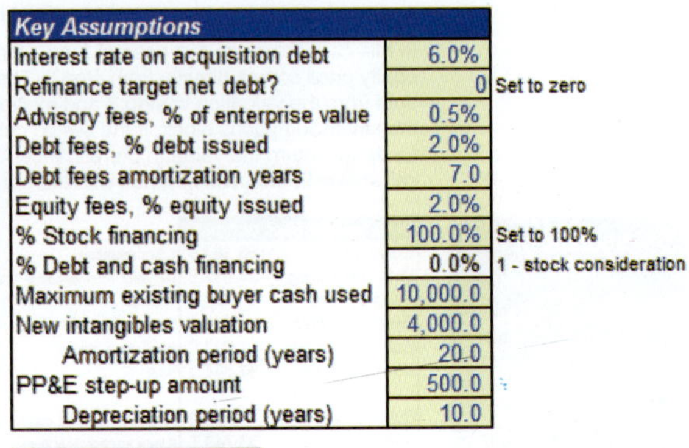

Key Assumptions		
Interest rate on acquisition debt	6.0%	
Refinance target net debt?	0	Set to zero
Advisory fees, % of enterprise value	0.5%	
Debt fees, % debt issued	2.0%	
Debt fees amortization years	7.0	
Equity fees, % equity issued	2.0%	
% Stock financing	100.0%	Set to 100%
% Debt and cash financing	0.0%	1 - stock consideration
Maximum existing buyer cash used	10,000.0	
New intangibles valuation	4,000.0	
Amortization period (years)	20.0	
PP&E step-up amount	500.0	
Depreciation period (years)	10.0	

Sources and Uses of Funds		
Equity price	68,183.5	From valuation
Debt refinancing	0.0	Net debt from valuation * switch
Advisory fees	463.6	% of EV
Debt issue fees	0.0	% of debt issued
Equity issue fees	1,363.7	% of stock issued
Uses of funds	**70,010.8**	Sum
Buyer's cash	1,827.3	MIN(Cash needed, cash available)
Debt issuance	0.0	(Uses except debt fees - cash - stock issue) / (1 - debt fee %)
Stock issuance	68,183.5	% Stock * equity purchase price
Sources of funds	**70,010.8**	Sum

Step 6 - calculate goodwill

FX issues...

The target data may need to be converted into the buyer currency using an exchange rate

The goodwill calculation takes the price paid for the equity and compares it with the shareholders' equity purchased. The shareholders' equity purchased is represented by the assets and liabilities of the target business so some calculations use net assets (total assets less total liabilities) while others use shareholders' equity. The fundamental accounting equation means that they are, by definition, the same number.

Total assets - total liabilities = Shareholders' equity

In theory, the net assets (or shareholders' equity) should be included at fair value but in a quick and dirty model it is easiest to assume that book amount equals fair value. This means that the values from the latest available balance sheet are used in the goodwill calculation with one exception. The value of any goodwill amount in the target balance sheet is always reduced to zero. This is because goodwill is not an "identifiable" asset since it cannot be bought or sold in its own right. This means that its value, when separately identified must be zero.

The process of reducing the target net assets by the amount of target goodwill simply makes the deal goodwill increase by the same amount. In practice, this means that the target goodwill is simply re-categorized as deal goodwill. This will be significant in any situation where goodwill amortization is calculated. This is the case, in some countries, where this goodwill is tax deductible on an amortized basis.

In this model, target goodwill is reduced to zero as explained above. Also both the PP&E and the intangibles are being stepped up. When assets are stepped up a deferred tax liability is also created. More detail on the deferred tax impact of acquisitions can be found in the section called *Goodwill and asset step-ups* on page 75.

Always check...

Target existing goodwill and reduce to zero to consolidate. Step-up information may need to come from your client

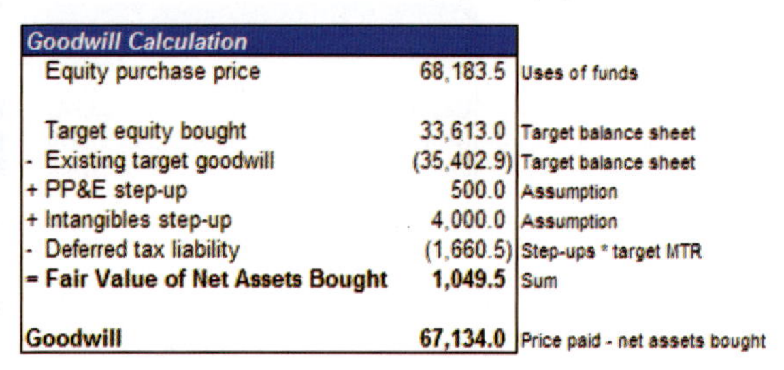

Goodwill Calculation		
Equity purchase price	68,183.5	Uses of funds
Target equity bought	33,613.0	Target balance sheet
- Existing target goodwill	(35,402.9)	Target balance sheet
+ PP&E step-up	500.0	Assumption
+ Intangibles step-up	4,000.0	Assumption
- Deferred tax liability	(1,660.5)	Step-ups * target MTR
= Fair Value of Net Assets Bought	**1,049.5**	Sum
Goodwill	**67,134.0**	Price paid - net assets bought

Step 7 - forecast any asset step-ups going forward

If you make a fair value change to the balance sheet as a result of the goodwill calculation then the implications for the forward looking forecast must be considered. In respect of PP&E and intangibles, for example, any additional depreciation and amortization should be added to the forecast.

Fair Value Adjustments	XX	XY	XZ	
Beginning PP&E step-up		500.0	450.0	Last year's ending
Depreciation		(50.0)	(50.0)	Step-up / life assumption
Ending PP&E step-up	500.0	450.0	400.0	Sum
Beginning intangibles step-up		4,000.0	3,800.0	Last year's ending
Amortization		(200.0)	(200.0)	Step-up / life assumption
Ending intangibles step-up	4,000.0	3,800.0	3,600.0	Sum

Step 8 - forecast the tax impact of any asset step-ups going forward

As the assets are reduced in the balance sheet by the process of depreciation and amortization in step 7 above, the associated deferred tax liability must be reduced in tandem.

Deferred Tax Impact	XX	XY	XZ	
Beginning deferred tax liability		1,660.5	1,568.3	Last year's ending
Reversal		(92.3)	(92.3)	D&A * target MTR
Ending deferred tax liability	1,660.5	1,568.3	1,476.0	Sum

Step 9 - forecast deal debt going forward

New debt is likely to be used to finance some or all of the deal. This debt, its repayment schedule and interest must be calculated for the forecast period.

Acquisition Debt	XX	XY	XZ	
Scheduled repayments		1,000.0	1,000.0	
Beginning debt		33,749.7	32,749.7	Last year's ending
Repayment		(1,000.0)	(1,000.0)	Repayment assumption
Ending debt	33,749.7	32,749.7	31,749.7	Sum
Interest expense		1,995.0	1,935.0	Average balance * rate

Step 10 - forecast amortization of deal debt fees going forward

Debt fees are paid when the debt is issued but expensed over the life of the loan, consequently a prepaid asset is created in the balance sheet. This prepaid asset is shown as a deduction against the debt balance under IFRS but may be presented as an asset under US GAAP. Whichever convention is followed, from a modeling perspective, it is best to include it as a separate line item in the balance sheet so that it is clearly visible.

Debt Issuance Fees	XX	XY	XZ	
Beginning deal debt fees		675.0	578.6	Last year's ending
Amortization		(96.4)	(96.4)	Fees / life assumption
Ending deal debt fees	675.0	578.6	482.1	Sum

Step 11 - calculate consolidated DSO

Pay attention...

It is very easy to use an incorrect share price when calculating the number of shares to be issued - it must be the buyer share price

If equity is being issued to do the deal then the consolidated DSO will be bigger than the current standalone DSO of the buyer. Start with the current DSO of the buyer and increase it by the number of shares that must be issued to do the deal. This is calculated by taking the money amount of equity to be issued (from the sources of funds calculation in step 5) and divide it by the buyer share price. This gives the number of shares that will be issued. This should be done for the forecast period as shown below.

Combo Shares Calculations	XY	XZ	
Basic shares outstanding	3,257.0	3,257.0	From step 2
New shares issued	934.0	934.0	Equity issued / BUY share price
Combo WASO (basic)	**4,191.0**	**4,191.0**	Sum
Diluted shares outstanding	3,269.6	3,269.6	From step 2
New shares issued	934.0	934.0	Equity issued / BUY share price
Combo WASO (diluted)	**4,203.6**	**4,203.6**	Sum

Step 12 - consolidate the proforma balance sheet

	Buyer XX	Target XX	Adj.	Combo XX	
Assets					
Cash	16,246.0	2,320.2	(12,320.2)	6,246.0	BUY + TGT * refinancing switch - cash spent
OCA	22,748.0	12,849.6		35,597.6	BUY + TGT
Net PP&E	21,438.0	12,898.3	500.0	34,836.3	BUY + TGT + step-up
Goodwill	27,031.0	35,402.9	31,731.1	94,165.0	BUY + TGT - TGT + new
Intangibles	7,728.0	24,280.6	4,000.0	36,008.6	BUY + TGT + step-up
Other assets	16,447.0	1,362.6		17,809.6	BUY + TGT
Total Assets	**111,638.0**	**89,114.3**		**224,663.1**	
Liabilities					
Short-term debt	12,617.0	1,744.1	(1,744.1)	12,617.0	BUY + TGT - TGT * refinancing switch
OCL	17,526.0	12,901.1		30,427.1	BUY + TGT
OLTL	11,414.0	15,737.5	1,660.5	28,812.0	BUY + TGT + tax on step-up
Long-term debt	7,483.0	25,118.5	8,631.2	41,232.7	BUY + TGT + new - TGT * refinancing switch
Debt fees	0.0	0.0	(675.0)	(675.0)	Debt fees
Total Liabs.	**49,040.0**	**55,501.3**		**112,413.8**	
Equity					
Capital	347.0	18,070.9	32,044.0	50,461.9	BUY + TGT - TGT + new - fees
RE	62,251.0	15,542.1	(16,005.7)	61,787.4	BUY + TGT - TGT - fees
Total Equity	**62,598.0**	**33,613.0**		**112,249.3**	
Total L & E	**111,638.0**	**89,114.3**		**224,663.1**	
Balance?	***OK***	***OK***		***OK***	

Consolidating any line item involves the following process:

Buyer + Target + / - Deal changes = Combo

So the trick is to understand the deal changes before doing the consolidation. All deal changes will come from one of two sources in the model and so should be reviewed before starting. The sources and uses table (step 5) and the goodwill calculations (step 6) are the "go to" areas of the model.

The deal changes in the example above - from top to bottom - are as follows:

- The buyer's cash could be used to finance the transaction as identified in the sources of funds. The target's cash could be used to pay down its debt as part of any refinancing. A switch is used to model any debt financing impact
- PP&E step-up from the goodwill calculation
- Deal goodwill less the target goodwill reduced to zero both come from the goodwill calculation
- Intangibles step-up from the goodwill calculation
- Short-term debt may be refinanced and therefore a switch must be used
- Deferred tax liability step-up from the goodwill calculation

Debt issued is from the sources of funds. Any change in the target's debt as a result of refinancing is modeled using a switch

- Unamortized debt issuance fees which may be shown as a prepaid asset under US GAPP
- Equity is adjusted for any equity issued less issuance fees (linked from the sources of funds). The target's equity (from the goodwill calculation) is always deducted on consolidation
- Retained earnings of the target are reduced to zero and the advisory fees are deducted

It is vital to note that every line item in both the sources and uses and the goodwill calculation is a deal change in the consolidated balance sheet.

Don't forget...

Fees...if omitted the consolidated balance sheet will not balance by that amount

The accounting for fees varies by fee type. The categories of fees are:

- Equity issuance fees
- Debt issuance fees
- Advisory fees

Equity issuance fees are deducted from additional paid in capital / share premium account. In most models, this means the capital or equity line item (since bankers typically add common stock and additional paid in capital together).

Debt issuance fees are deducted from the debt raised (IFRS) or are shown as a prepaid asset (US GAAP) on the balance sheet. These fees are amortized into the income statement / profit and loss account over the life of the debt. The amortization expense is reported as part of the interest cost so will impact net income and earnings per share. There will be no impact on EBIT or EBITDA.

Advisory fees on the other hand are expensed in the first year post year. This means that reported operating profit is reduced by the advisory fees. Reported net income is reduced by the advisory fees net of any tax. EBIT and EBITDA are unlikely to be impacted since the advisory fees will almost certainly be treated as a non-recurring item by analysts. It is likely that recurring net income will also be cleaned of the post-tax advisory fees.

This means that EBIT, EBITDA, net income and earnings per share are affected, unless they have been cleaned for this "non-recurring" expense. The treatment of advisory fees is a change from the previous accounting treatment where they were added to the purchase price and capitalized as part of goodwill.

In this model the advisory fees have been deducted from retained earnings as a simplified approach. Also, it is assumed the fees are not tax deductible (which is often the case). In reality, a prepaid asset should be set up which is transferred into the income statement / profit and loss in the first year post deal. Care will need to be taken regarding the tax deductibility of these fees.

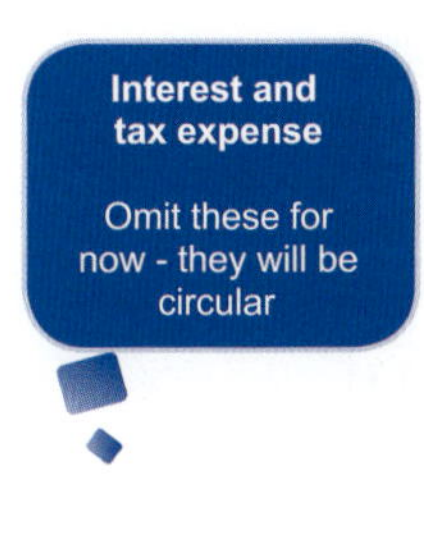

Step 13 - build the consolidated income statement / profit and loss except for interest and tax expense

Income Statement	XY	XZ	
Net sales	135,831.8	142,344.5	BUY + TGT
COGS	(71,486.8)	(74,594.7)	BUY + TGT
Depreciation	(3,934.0)	(4,182.0)	BUY + TGT + depn. on step-up
Gross profit	**60,411.0**	**63,567.8**	
SG&A	(38,879.5)	(40,703.5)	BUY + TGT - synergies
Amortization	(1,035.7)	(1,035.7)	BUY + TGT + amort. on step-up
EBIT	**20,495.8**	**21,828.5**	
EBITDA	**25,465.5**	**27,046.3**	EBIT + D&A
Non-recurring income / (expense)	(379.7)	(358.2)	BUY + TGT
Other income / (expense)	700.0	700.0	BUY + TGT
Interest expense, net			Leave for now
Profit before taxes	**20,816.1**	**22,170.3**	
Tax expense			Leave for now
Net income	**20,816.1**	**22,170.3**	
Post tax non-recurring items	239.6	226.0	BUY + TGT
Normalized net income	**21,055.7**	**22,396.3**	
Dividends	12,489.7	13,302.2	Calc. using assumption
Shareholder information			
Basic WASO	4,191.0	4,191.0	From step 11
Diluted WASO	4,203.6	4,203.6	From step 11
Earnings per share - Basic	5.02	5.34	Normalized NI / Basic SO
Earnings per share - Diluted	5.01	5.33	Normalized NI / DSO
Cash EPS - Diluted	5.06	5.38	Normalized NI + extra D&A / DSO
Dividends per share	2.98	3.17	Calc. using assumption

As before, the consolidation process is as follows:

Buyer + Target + / - Deal changes = Combo

The key focus is to understand the deal changes that will impact the year on year income statement / profit and loss account.

The deal changes in the example above - from top to bottom - are as follows:

- Extra depreciation driven by the PP&E step-up
- Synergies impacting SG&A
- Extra depreciation driven by the intangibles step-up
- Interest impact of deal financing (not calculated until step 17)
- Tax impact of all deal changes (not calculated until step 18)

The interest and tax line items are left blank for now because they will cause circular references. To include them at this stage would necessitate turning on iteration to deal with them. This means that Excel would calculate through any further circular references whether unintentional or not and this is not desirable yet.

Earnings per share is calculated as normal but in this case "Cash EPS" has also been calculated. This excludes the incremental non-cash items such as depreciation and amortization from asset step-ups.

Step 14 - build the consolidated balance sheet except for cash plug items

Balance Sheet	XX	XY	
Assets			
Cash and cash equivalents	6,246.0		Leave for now
Non-cash current assets	35,597.6	36,147.7	BUY + TGT
Net PP&E	34,836.3	36,920.0	BUY + TGT + step-up
Goodwill	94,165.0	94,165.0	BUY + TGT - TGT + new
Identifiable intangible assets	36,008.6	34,972.9	BUY + TGT + step-up
Other assets	17,809.6	18,139.8	BUY + TGT
Total Assets	**224,663.1**	**220,345.4**	
Liabilities			
Short-term debt	12,617.0		Leave for now
Non-debt current liabilities	30,427.1	30,706.3	BUY + TGT
Other long-term liabilities	28,812.0	28,676.4	BUY + TGT + tax on step-up
Long-term debt	41,232.7	40,232.7	BUY + TGT + new - TGT * ?
Unamortized debt issuance fees	(675.0)	(578.6)	Amortized debt fees
Total Liabilities	**112,413.8**	**99,036.9**	
Equity			
Capital	50,461.9	50,461.9	BUY + new - fees
Retained earnings	61,787.4	70,113.8	Beginning + NI - dividends
Total Equity	**112,249.3**	**120,575.7**	
Total Liabilities & Equity	**224,663.1**	**219,612.6**	
Balance?	***0.0***	***(732.8)***	

The normal consolidation process applies when building the consolidated balance sheet:

Buyer + Target + / - Deal changes = Combo

The cash plug items (cash and cash equivalents and short-term debt in this case) are best sourced from the cash flow statement as for a normal three statement model.

The only line item that is problematic using the normal consolidation process is retained earnings. Retained earnings is a cumulative number and therefore the income deal changes (which affect it) need to be done cumulatively. This becomes prohibitive as you move forward in time. Luckily using a simple BASE analysis solves the problem. It take the retained earnings from the prior period consolidated balance sheet, adds on consolidated net income from the income statement / profit and loss and deducts the consolidated dividends.

Good news...

This is largely the same as a normal cash flow statement build. If some data is not easily available then consolidate that line item

Step 15 - build the consolidated cash flow statement

Cash Flow Statement	XX	XY	XZ	
Net income		20,816.1	22,170.3	From IS
+ Depreciation		3,934.0	4,182.0	From IS
+ Amortization		1,035.7	1,035.7	From IS
+ Amortization of debt issuance fees		96.4	96.4	This yr. BS - last yr. BS
(Inc) Dec in operating working capital		(270.9)	(290.5)	Last yr. BS - this yr. BS
Inc (Dec) other long-term liabilities		(135.6)	521.8	This yr. BS - last yr. BS
(Inc) Dec in other assets		(330.2)	(62.6)	Last yr. BS - this yr. BS
Cash flow from operations		**25,145.6**	**27,653.1**	
Capital expenditure		(6,017.7)	(6,314.7)	BUY + TGT
Cash flow from investing		**(6,017.7)**	**(6,314.7)**	
Inc (Dec) in long-term debt		(1,000.0)	(1,000.0)	This yr. BS - last yr. BS
Inc (Dec) in capital		0.0	0.0	This yr. BS - last yr. BS
Dividends		(12,489.7)	(13,302.2)	From step 13
Cash flow from financing		**(13,489.7)**	**(14,302.2)**	
Net cash flow		**5,638.2**	**7,036.2**	
Cash / (short-term debt)	(6,371.0)	(732.8)	6,303.3	Beginning + NCF

The construction of any cash flow statement requires two balance sheets, one income statement / profit and loss and some supplementary information. The consolidated balance sheets and income statement / profit and loss have already been prepared, allowing the majority of the consolidated cash flow statement to be prepared. The only cash flow item that needs a "consolidation" approach is capital expenditure since this data is unavailable in the income statement / profit and loss or balance sheet.

It balances!!

If it doesn't - do not continue - stop and investigate. Check from the sources and uses and goodwill calculations to the deal changes

Step 16 - plug the cash numbers from the cash flow statement into the balance sheet

Balance Sheet	XX	XY	
Assets			
Cash and cash equivalents	6,246.0	0.0	MAX(Cash from CFS,0)
Non-cash current assets	35,597.6	36,147.7	BUY + TGT
Net PP&E	34,836.3	36,920.0	BUY + TGT + step-up
Goodwill	94,165.0	94,165.0	BUY + TGT - TGT + new
Identifiable intangible assets	36,008.6	34,972.9	BUY + TGT + step-up
Other assets	17,809.6	18,139.8	BUY + TGT
Total Assets	**224,663.1**	**220,345.4**	
Liabilities			
Short-term debt	12,617.0	732.8	MIN(Cash from CFS,0) * - 1
Non-debt current liabilities	30,427.1	30,706.3	BUY + TGT
Other long-term liabilities	28,812.0	28,676.4	BUY + TGT + tax on step-up
Long-term debt	41,232.7	40,232.7	BUY + TGT + new - TGT * ?
Unamortized debt issuance fees	(675.0)	(578.6)	Amortized debt fees
Total Liabilities	**112,413.8**	**99,769.7**	
Equity			
Capital	50,461.9	50,461.9	BUY + new - fees
Retained earnings	61,787.4	70,113.8	Beginning + NI - dividends
Total Equity	**112,249.3**	**120,575.7**	
Total Liabilities & Equity	**224,663.1**	**220,345.4**	
Balance?	***0.0***	***0.0***	

At this stage the cash flow number is plugged into the balance sheet. If it is a positive number then it will be shown as cash and cash equivalents as part of current assets. The formula is as follows:

MAX (Ending cash from CFS, 0)

If it is a negative number, this implies a financing shortfall which must be plugged with debt - for example using a revolving credit facility. In this case short-term debt will be populated with the following formula:

MIN (Ending cash from CFS, 0) * -1

If it does not balance at this stage, then there is an error which should be found before progressing. Continuing to build the model knowing there are errors is likely to cause more problems. Since the proforma balance sheet balanced something must be wrong with the first year forecast numbers so these should all be checked in detail.

Step 17 - calculate consolidated interest

Net Interest Expense	XY	XZ	
Buyer interest expense on LT debt	(299.3)	(299.3)	BUY
Target interest expense on LT debt	0.0	0.0	TGT * (1 - refinancing switch)
Deal debt interest expense	(1,995.0)	(1,935.0)	From step 9
Amortization of debt issuance fees	(96.4)	(96.4)	From step 10
Interest expense on combo ST debt	(166.9)	(9.2)	Rate * average Combo ST debt
Interest income on combo cash	46.8	47.3	Rate * average Combo cash
Total net interest expense	**(2,510.8)**	**(2,292.6)**	
Net cash interest expense	(2,414.3)	(2,196.2)	Total - amortization of debt fees
Additional interest expense	(986.7)	(991.9)	Total - sum (BUY + TGT)

The consolidated interest is a secondary calculation which should be built in stages for simplicity. The standalone interest on long-term debt is linked from the underlying forecasts for the buyer and the target. The target interest should be linked using the refinancing switch. The interest expense and debt issuance fees on newly issued deal debt have already been calculated in steps 9 and 10 and can be linked to the calculations here.

The interest income on cash and interest expense on short-term debt are calculated as the interest on average consolidated balances per a normal forecast model. In this model the buyer standalone interest rates have been used. If this is inappropriate, new assumptions should be made. This method avoids having to list out the deal changes that impact these line items.

Frequently a supplementary calculation of "cash interest" is performed. This is used for credit metrics and is very important in cases where interest is PIK (paid in kind). In this case the only item which is not cash is the amortization of the debt issuance fees.

Finally, the incremental interest calculates the variance between consolidated interest expense and the sum of the standalone interest expenses. This shows the total impact on interest of the deal itself without breaking it down into the component parts.

Step 18 - calculate consolidated tax expense

Tax Expense	XY	XZ	
Buyer tax expense	(4,111.2)	(4,319.4)	BUY
Target tax expense	(1,978.9)	(2,150.9)	TGT
Tax on synergies	(36.9)	(73.8)	Synergies * MTR
Tax shield on fair value adjustments	92.3	92.3	From step 8
Tax shield on additional interest expense	635.2	580.0	From step 17 * MTR
Total tax expense	**(5,399.6)**	**(5,871.9)**	

In principle, this can be done in two ways. The quick way is to take the consolidated profit before tax and apply an appropriate MTR. This works well in situations where the MTR is reasonably consistent between the buyer and the target.

The other methodology (used above) uses the standard consolidation principles:

Buyer + Target + / - Deal changes = Combo

Care should be taken to identify the deal changes in the first instance and then to ensure that the direction of the adjustment is correct (this is very easy to get wrong). In this case, the first deal change is the increased tax expense caused by the impact of synergies. The correct MTR should also be used. Most of the time, it is assumed that the majority of synergies will be made at the target level which means the target MTR is appropriate. Synergies will increase profit before tax, therefore tax expense will increase.

The tax shield on the fair value adjustments comes from the deferred tax calculation done in step 8 above. The extra D&A has reduced consolidated profit before tax which in turn should reduce the tax expense. However, this has not happened because consolidated profit before tax has not been used to build the tax expense calculation. This adjustment captures the tax impact of the incremental D&A.

Finally, the tax impact of the incremental interest is included. The incremental interest was calculated in step 17 so the MTR should be applied to calculate the tax impact. Normally the MTR of the buyer is used but this assumes that the financing is done at the buyer level which may not be the case. It is possible to break this piece down into its component parts so that different MTRs can be used however, this is not easy and care should be taken to avoid doing a lot of work which results in a similar answer. The use of the buyer MTR is normally appropriate especially since it gives a reasonable answer and is simple to calculate.

Step 19 - include interest and tax expense in the income statement / profit and loss using a circular switch

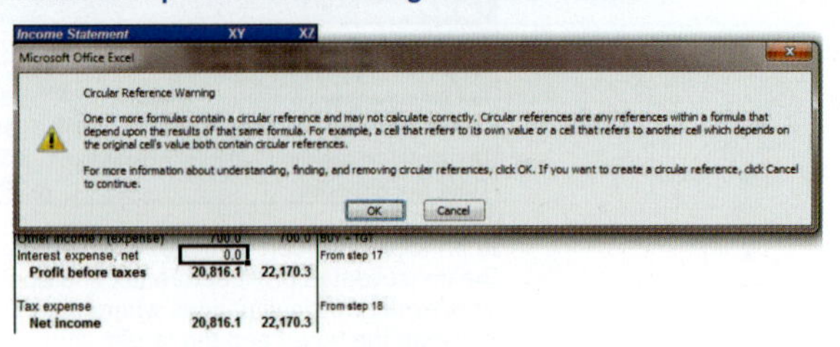

When interest is included in the income statement / profit and loss, a dialogue box will open warning that the model now has a circular reference and that Excel cannot calculate it because iteration has been turned off. Cancel this warning (if OK is hit several help messages appear, none of which are helpful in this context).

When the message is cancelled the interest expense will be populated with a zero value and also the status bar will show a circular reference warning with a cell reference visible.

Now link in the tax expense which is also circular due to the incremental interest line of the calculation. Again this will be populated with a zero value indicating that this is part of a circular reference also.

Income Statement	XY	XZ	
Net sales	135,831.8	142,344.5	BUY + TGT
COGS	(71,486.8)	(74,594.7)	BUY + TGT
Depreciation	(3,934.0)	(4,182.0)	BUY + TGT + depn. on step-up
Gross profit	**60,411.0**	**63,567.8**	
SG&A	(38,879.5)	(40,703.5)	BUY + TGT - synergies
Amortization	(1,035.7)	(1,035.7)	BUY + TGT + amort. on step-up
EBIT	**20,495.8**	**21,828.5**	
EBITDA	**25,465.5**	**27,046.3**	EBIT + D&A
Non-recurring income / (expense)	(379.7)	(358.2)	BUY + TGT
Other income / (expense)	700.0	700.0	BUY + TGT
Interest expense, net	0.0	0.0	From step 17
Profit before taxes	**20,816.1**	**22,170.3**	
Tax expense	0.0	0.0	From step 18
Net income	**20,816.1**	**22,170.3**	

Turn on Excel's iteration functionality as shown below. This enables Excel to calculate through the circularity and return a value in both the interest expense and tax lines as shown below.

Iteration
If using Excel 2003, this is found in Tools Options Iteration

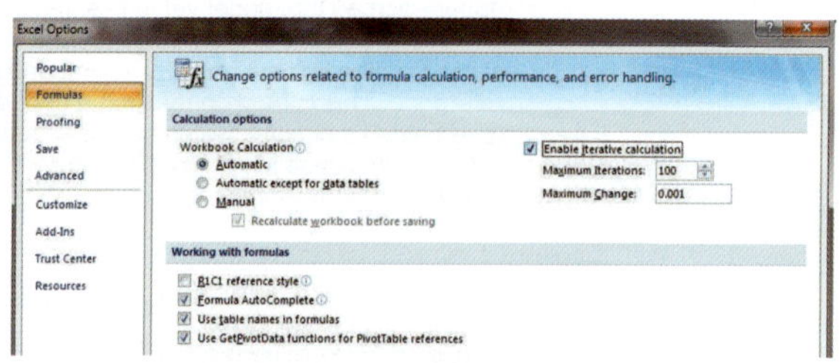

Income Statement	XY	XZ	
Net sales	135,831.8	142,344.5	BUY + TGT
COGS	(71,486.8)	(74,594.7)	BUY + TGT
Depreciation	(3,934.0)	(4,182.0)	BUY + TGT + depn. on step-up
Gross profit	**60,411.0**	**63,567.8**	
SG&A	(38,879.5)	(40,703.5)	BUY + TGT - synergies
Amortization	(1,035.7)	(1,035.7)	BUY + TGT + amort. on step-up
EBIT	**20,495.8**	**21,828.5**	
EBITDA	**25,465.5**	**27,046.3**	EBIT + D&A
Non-recurring income / (expense)	(379.7)	(358.2)	BUY + TGT
Other income / (expense)	700.0	700.0	BUY + TGT
Interest expense, net	(2,550.5)	(2,381.7)	From step 17
Profit before taxes	**18,265.6**	**19,788.7**	
Tax expense	(5,389.5)	(5,849.4)	From step 18
Net income	**12,876.1**	**13,939.3**	

It should be noted that the process of iteration has actually changed the numbers. The interest and tax expense as calculated in step 17 is now producing a slightly different result due to the iterative process. The new numbers shown in the income statement / profit and loss above are consistent with the updated secondary calculations as shown below.

Net Interest Expense	XY	XZ	
Buyer interest expense on LT debt	(299.3)	(299.3)	BUY
Target interest expense on LT debt	0.0	0.0	TGT * ?
Deal debt interest expense	(1,995.0)	(1,935.0)	From step 9
Amortization of debt issuance fees	(96.4)	(96.4)	From step 10
Interest expense on combo ST debt	(206.6)	(50.9)	Rate * average Combo ST debt
Interest income on combo cash	46.8	0.0	Rate * average Combo cash
Total net interest expense	**(2,550.5)**	**(2,381.7)**	
Net cash interest expense	(2,454.0)	(2,285.2)	Total - amortization of debt fees
Additional interest expense	(2,550.5)	(2,381.7)	Total - sum (BUY + TGT)

Tax Expense	XY	XZ	
Buyer tax expense	(4,111.2)	(4,319.4)	BUY
Target tax expense	(1,978.9)	(2,150.9)	TGT
Tax on synergies	(36.9)	(73.8)	Synergies * MTR
Tax shield on fair value adjustments	92.3	92.3	From step 8
Tax shield on additional interest exp.	645.3	602.6	From step 17 * MTR
Total tax expense	**(5,389.5)**	**(5,849.4)**	

The problem now is that the existence of the circular references means that this model is now unstable and may "blow up". When a model suffers a "blow up", REF, VALUE or NAME error messages appear across the model yet in this instance there is no error. The only way to solve the problem is to remove the circular reference, allow Excel to solve a linear problem, and then reinstate the circular reference. This is best done using a circular switch. In this model (see below) a circular switch has been set up which is range-named "Circ". In this case simply multiplying by the switch will not remove the circular nature of the formula so an IF statement must be used as follows:

IF (Circ = 1, interest expense, 0)

IF (Circ = 1, tax expense, 0)

In the example below the circ switch is set to zero so interest expense returns an absolute zero value which is not the result of a circular formula.

Income Statement	XY	XZ	
Net sales	135,831.8	142,344.5	BUY + TGT
COGS	(71,486.8)	(74,594.7)	BUY + TGT
Depreciation	(3,934.0)	(4,182.0)	BUY + TGT + depn. on step-up
Gross profit	**60,411.0**	**63,567.8**	
SG&A	(38,879.5)	(40,703.5)	BUY + TGT - synergies
Amortization	(1,035.7)	(1,035.7)	BUY + TGT + amort. on step-up
EBIT	**20,495.8**	**21,828.5**	
EBITDA	**25,465.5**	**27,046.3**	EBIT + D&A
Non-recurring income / (expense)	(379.7)	(358.2)	BUY + TGT
Other income / (expense)	700.0	700.0	BUY + TGT
Interest expense, net	0.0	0.0	IF(Circ = 1, interest expense,0)
Profit before taxes	**20,816.1**	**22,170.3**	
Tax expense	0.0	0.0	IF(Circ = 1, tax expense,0)
Net income	**20,816.1**	**22,170.3**	

The final step is to set the circ switch to 1 (normally in the model documentation section) which means that the circular references will populate.

Model information:	
Analyst name:	<Analyst Name>
Date last modified:	<Date>
Number of circularities:	7
Sources:	Interest income (acquirer, target and combo)
	Interest expense (acquirer, target and combo)
	Tax expense (combo)
Circular switch:	1

Income Statement	XY	XZ	
Net sales	135,831.8	142,344.5	BUY + TGT
COGS	(71,486.8)	(74,594.7)	BUY + TGT
Depreciation	(3,934.0)	(4,182.0)	BUY + TGT + depn. on step-up
Gross profit	**60,411.0**	**63,567.8**	
SG&A	(38,879.5)	(40,703.5)	BUY + TGT - synergies
Amortization	(1,035.7)	(1,035.7)	BUY + TGT + amort. on step-up
EBIT	**20,495.8**	**21,828.5**	
EBITDA	**25,465.5**	**27,046.3**	EBIT + D&A
Non-recurring income / (expense)	(379.7)	(358.2)	BUY + TGT
Other income / (expense)	700.0	700.0	BUY + TGT
Interest expense, net	(2,550.0)	(2,380.4)	IF(Circ = 1, interest expense,0)
Profit before taxes	**18,266.1**	**19,790.0**	
Tax expense	(5,301.1)	(5,772.3)	IF(Circ = 1, tax expense,0)
Net income	**12,965.0**	**14,017.6**	

The model is now complete so the analysis can begin.

Merger consequences analysis

The main difference in the fully integrated merger model is that more analysis can be done on the affordability of the proposed financing structure. This is mainly because of the detailed balance sheet and cash flow forecasts that are produced by the model. All the analysis done using the quick and dirty model can be performed with the added advantage of being able to see the development of the metrics over time. This can be very useful.

- EPS accretion / dilution
- Synergies to breakeven
- Relative PEs
- Ownership dilution
- Contribution analysis
- Side by side comparison
- Analysis at various prices
- Return on invested capital - development over time
- Premium analysis - development over time
- Credit analysis - including affordability of new financing structure

Merger consequences analysis - EPS accretion / dilution

EPS accretion / dilution is widely used in deal analysis. It shows the extent to which EPS will increase or decrease as a result of the deal.

Naturally, it is purely earnings focused, and ignores key items such as the cost of any equity issued. Its narrow focus means that EPS accretion / dilution should not be used in isolation. A deal that is EPS accretive may not necessarily be a good deal.

Finally, if your analysis suggests that the deal is highly accretive, as is the case here, then it is important to ask if there are some other reasons why such a deal has not been done or attempted already. There might be issues associated with competition authorities or some such which makes a deal less attractive to a buyer.

EPS Acc. / Dil.	XY E	XZ E	
Buyer normalized EPS	3.17	3.35	BUY forecast
Combo normalized EPS	3.14	3.39	From step 13
EPS Acc. / dil.	**(1.0%)**	**1.1%**	(Combo EPS / BUY EPS) -1
Synergies to breakeven	211.8	0.0	(BUY EPS - Combo EPS) * combo DSO / (1 - MTR)
Buyer normalized EPS	3.17	3.35	BUY forecast
Combo Cash EPS	3.20	3.44	From step 13
EPS Acc. / dil.	**0.7%**	**2.7%**	(Combo EPS / BUY EPS) -1
Synergies to breakeven	0.0	0.0	(BUY EPS - Combo EPS) * combo DSO / (1 - MTR)

Merger consequences analysis - synergies to breakeven

This calculates the additional synergies needed to achieve zero EPS accretion / dilution. In this case, the deal is already accretive for cash EPS using the given assumptions, so no additional synergies are required to breakeven. For normalized EPS synergies are required to breakeven.

Building this calculation up in stages, the first stage is to calculate the EPS needed to achieve breakeven. This is:

Buyer standalone EPS - Consolidated EPS

However, it is unusual in the context of a deal to reference synergies on a per share basis so the next stage grosses this up as follows:

(Buyer standalone EPS - Consolidated EPS) * Consolidated DSO

This gives a gross number, based on net income, which is a post-tax number but it is more common to reference pre-tax numbers for synergies so it must be grossed up for tax:

$$\frac{\text{(Buyer standalone EPS - Consolidated EPS) * Consolidate DSO}}{\text{(1 - MTR)}}$$

Finally, if the deal is accretive already then the answer to this calculation is zero. The formula above will give a negative result which is mathematically correct but does not make sense. An easy fix is to wrap this formula within a MAX function which compares it to zero. The final version becomes:

$$\text{MAX}\left[\frac{\text{(Buyer standalone EPS - Consolidated EPS) * Consolidate DSO}}{\text{(1 - MTR)}}, 0\right]$$

This can be stress tested by changing assumptions so that the deal is very dilutive, in this case, change the deal so it is 100% stock financed. This means no debt or balance sheet cash is being used. Setting the synergy assumption to zero also means this calculation will give the total (rather than additional) synergies to breakeven.

Key Assumptions		
% Stock financing	100.0%	Set at 100%
% Debt and cash financing	0.0%	1 - stock consideration
Maximum existing buyer cash used	0.0	Set to zero
New intangibles valuation	4,000.0	
Amortization period (years)	20.0	
PP&E step-up amount	500.0	
Depreciation period (years)	10.0	

Breakeven synergies...

It is useful to sanity check how achievable synergies are by using comparable transaction data

Synergy Assumptions	XY	XZ	
SG&A synergy forecast	0.0	0.0	Set to zero
Combo SG&A pre-syn.	38,979.5	40,903.5	BUY + TGT
Combo Sales pre-syn.	135,831.8	142,344.5	BUY + TGT
Synergy forecast %	0.0%	0.0%	Synergies % SG&A
Synergy forecast %	0.0%	0.0%	Synergies % Sales

EPS Acc. / Dil.	XY E	XZ E	
Buyer normalized EPS	3.17	3.35	BUY forecast
Combo normalized EPS	3.01	3.23	From step 13
EPS Acc. / dil.	**(5.1%)**	**(3.8%)**	(Combo EPS / BUY EPS) -1
Synergies to breakeven	1,166.5	903.2	(BUY EPS - Combo EPS) * combo DSO / (1 - MTR)
Buyer normalized EPS	3.17	3.35	BUY forecast
Combo Cash EPS	3.06	3.27	From step 13
EPS Acc. / dil.	**(3.6%)**	**(2.3%)**	(Combo EPS / BUY EPS) -1
Synergies to breakeven	825.5	562.2	(BUY EPS - Combo EPS) * combo DSO / (1 - MTR)

Next, copy and paste this value into the synergy assumption and the EPS accretion / dilution will be zero. If it is not, then the integrity of the model is questionable and needs to be checked in detail to identify the source of the error.

Key Assumptions		
% Stock financing	100.0%	Set at 100%
% Debt and cash financing	0.0%	1 - stock consideration
Maximum existing buyer cash used	0.0	Set to zero
New intangibles valuation	4,000.0	
Amortization period (years)	20.0	
PP&E step-up amount	500.0	
Depreciation period (years)	10.0	

Synergy Assumptions	XY	XZ	
SG&A synergy forecast	1,166.5	0.0	Copy and paste value
Combo SG&A pre-syn.	38,979.5	40,903.5	BUY + TGT
Combo Sales pre-syn.	135,831.8	142,344.5	BUY + TGT
Synergy forecast %	3.0%	0.0%	Synergies % SG&A
Synergy forecast %	0.9%	0.0%	Synergies % Sales

EPS Acc. / Dil.	XY E	XZ E	
Buyer normalized EPS	3.17	3.35	BUY forecast
Combo normalized EPS	3.17	3.23	From step 13
EPS Acc. / dil.	**0.0%**	**(3.7%)**	(Combo EPS / BUY EPS) -1
Synergies to breakeven	0.0	898.0	(BUY EPS - Combo EPS) * combo DSO / (1 - MTR)
Buyer normalized EPS	3.17	3.35	BUY forecast
Combo Cash EPS	3.22	3.27	From step 13
EPS Acc. / dil.	**1.5%**	**(2.3%)**	(Combo EPS / BUY EPS) -1
Synergies to breakeven	0.0	557.0	(BUY EPS - Combo EPS) * combo DSO / (1 - MTR)

Merger consequences analysis - relative PEs

Deal Analysis	XY E	XZ E	
Buyer P/E	17.3 x	16.3 x	BUY share price / BUY EPS
Acquisition P/E	18.5 x	16.6 x	Offer price / TGT EPS
Debt P/E	22.3 x	22.3 x	1 / post-tax cost of debt

A comparison of the buyer PE and the acquisition PE gives you a quick analysis of the deal. In the simplest situation of 100% stock or 100% cash deal with zero synergies, it will give you the same answer as EPS accretion / dilution. Consequently it should always be used as a stress test of the model.

The acquisition (or offer) PE gives an indication of the implied return on equity from this investment. It compares the prices being paid with the earnings being bought. If you calculate the inverse you will get the answer in % terms rather than multiple terms. In this example, the year 1 acquisition PE is 18.5 x which implies a 5.4% return on equity.

The return on equity should be compared to the cost of equity to establish whether or not it is sufficient. If the financing is all stock the implied cost equity is provided by the buyer PE. This gives us the market demand in earnings for every $ invested. Again, the inverse of the PE gives this data in percentage terms. In this case, the buyer PE in the first year is 17.3 x which implies a cost of stock financing of 5.8%.

An investment expected to yield 5.4% and financed with financing costing 5.8% is not, on the face of it, a good deal. This is easily seen by comparing the PEs. The buyer PE is lower than the acquisition PE, which means that the cost of raising buyer equity is higher than return expected from the target equity being purchased. The buyer PE needs to be higher than the acquisition PE in order for the deal to be accretive. Since this analysis only uses the standalone numbers then incremental changes, such as synergies, are not taken into account.

If the assumptions are changed to 100% stock financing and zero synergies, the relative PEs and the EPS accretion / dilution give consistent results.

PE analysis…

If financing is all stock or all debt and synergies are zero then the PE analysis and the EPS accretion / dilution will be consistent… otherwise… check your model to establish why not

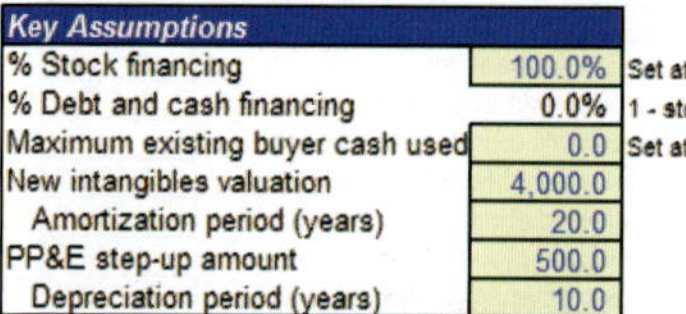

Key Assumptions		
% Stock financing	100.0%	Set at 100%
% Debt and cash financing	0.0%	1 - stock consideration
Maximum existing buyer cash used	0.0	Set at zero
New intangibles valuation	4,000.0	
Amortization period (years)	20.0	
PP&E step-up amount	500.0	
Depreciation period (years)	10.0	

Synergy Assumptions	XY	XZ	
SG&A synergy forecast	0.0	0.0	Set at zero
Combo SG&A pre-syn.	38,979.5	40,903.5	BUY + TGT
Combo Sales pre-syn.	135,831.8	142,344.5	BUY + TGT
Synergy forecast %	0.0%	0.0%	Synergies % SG&A
Synergy forecast %	0.0%	0.0%	Synergies % Sales

Deal Analysis	XY E	XZ E	
Buyer P/E	17.3 x	16.3 x	BUY share price / BUY EPS
Acquisition P/E	18.5 x	16.6 x	Offer price / TGT EPS
Debt P/E	22.3 x	22.3 x	1 / post-tax cost of debt

EPS Acc. / Dil.	XY E	XZ E	
Buyer normalized EPS	3.17	3.35	BUY forecast
Combo normalized EPS	3.01	3.23	From step 13
EPS Acc. / dil.	**(5.1%)**	**(3.8%)**	(Combo EPS / BUY EPS) -1
Synergies to breakeven	1,166.5	903.2	(BUY EPS - Combo EPS) * combo DSO / (1 - MTR)
Buyer normalized EPS	3.17	3.35	BUY forecast
Combo Cash EPS	3.06	3.27	From step 13
EPS Acc. / dil.	**(3.6%)**	**(2.3%)**	(Combo EPS / BUY EPS) -1
Synergies to breakeven	825.5	562.2	(BUY EPS - Combo EPS) * combo DSO / (1 - MTR)

But what if the financing were different? If cash is paid by issuing debt then the cost of financing is the post-tax cost of debt, in this case, 4.5%. This means that if the implied return on equity purchased is 5.4% and it is financed with debt costing 4.5%, it seems to be a viable deal. Running the numbers with 100% debt financing and zero synergies, this is exactly what is seen - an accretive deal.

Key Assumptions		
% Stock financing	0.0%	Set at zero
% Debt and cash financing	100.0%	1 - stock consideration
Maximum existing buyer cash used	0.0	Set at zero
New intangibles valuation	4,000.0	
Amortization period (years)	20.0	
PP&E step-up amount	500.0	
Depreciation period (years)	10.0	

Synergy Assumptions	XY	XZ	
SG&A synergy forecast	0.0	0.0	Set at zero
Combo SG&A pre-syn.	38,979.5	40,903.5	BUY + TGT
Combo Sales pre-syn.	135,831.8	142,344.5	BUY + TGT
Synergy forecast %	0.0%	0.0%	Synergies % SG&A
Synergy forecast %	0.0%	0.0%	Synergies % Sales

Deal Analysis	XY E	XZ E	
Buyer P/E	17.3 x	16.3 x	BUY share price / BUY EPS
Acquisition P/E	18.5 x	16.6 x	Offer price / TGT EPS
Debt P/E	22.3 x	22.3 x	1 / post-tax cost of debt

EPS Acc. / Dil.	XY E	XZ E	
Buyer normalized EPS	3.17	3.35	BUY forecast
Combo normalized EPS	3.18	3.47	From step 13
EPS Acc. / dil.	**0.1%**	**3.5%**	(Combo EPS / BUY EPS) -1
Synergies to breakeven	0.0	0.0	(BUY EPS - Combo EPS) * combo DSO / (1 - MTR)
Buyer normalized EPS	3.17	3.35	BUY forecast
Combo Cash EPS	3.29	3.58	From step 13
EPS Acc. / dil.	**3.6%**	**6.8%**	(Combo EPS / BUY EPS) -1
Synergies to breakeven	0.0	0.0	(BUY EPS - Combo EPS) * combo DSO / (1 - MTR)

If the deal were financed entirely with balance sheet cash, it is likely (all other things being equal) to be even more accretive since the post-tax interest income lost (cost of finance) is lower than the cost of the deal debt with an expected return on the equity bought of 5.4%.

It is more common, in the industry, to do this analysis using PEs rather than percentages. To calculate the "debt PE", simply take the inverse of the post-tax cost of debt. In this case this gives a multiple of 22.3 x. Similarly the "Cash PE" is the inverse of the post-tax lost interest income.

The PE of the financing must be higher than the offer PE in order to produce an accretive deal. In this case, the offer PE is higher than the buyer PE but lower than the debt and cash PEs which implies dilution if 100% stock financing is used but accretion if 100% debt / cash is used. When the model is stress tested using these assumptions and zero synergies this is, in fact, what is observed for EPS accretion / dilution. These stress tests should always be done in order to check the model is working as expected.

One final point, this check works very well at the financing extremes (100% stock or 100% debt) but does not predict well when a mix of financing is used. This is the reason why stress testing by changing the assumptions is critical to test the integrity of the model.

In summary:

If the buyer PE > offer PE the deal is likely to be accretive
If the buyer PE < offer PE the deal is likely to be dilutive
If the debt or cash PE > offer PE the deal is likely to be accretive
If the debt or cash PE < offer PE the deal is likely to be dilutive

A comparison of the buyer PE and the offer PE gives you a quick and dirty view of the deal. In the simplest situation of 100% stock or 100% cash deal with zero synergies, it will give you the same answer as EPS accretion / dilution. Consequently it should always be used as a stress test of the model, at the very least.

Merger consequences analysis - ownership dilution

This is important when some or all of the consideration is with stock. It shows the extent to which the buyer shareholders are "giving away" their ownership in the business to pay for the deal. The calculation is straightforward:

$$\frac{\text{Buyer DSO standalone}}{\text{Consolidated DSO}}$$

This shows the percentage ownership in the post-deal world. A key question for the deal team is to understand whether this will be acceptable to the buying shareholders.

Finally, this means we can calculate the exchange ratio. This is the number of buyer shares that a target shareholder will receive in exchange for shares in the target company.

$$\frac{\text{Buyer shares issued (from consolidated DSO calculation)}}{\text{Target shares purchased}}$$

Or:

$$\frac{\text{Offer price}}{\text{Buyer share price}} * \text{\% stock financing}$$

It is generally shown to four or five decimal places and is always communicated to the target shareholders in the offer document. In this case the selling shareholders will receive 0.5248 buyer shares and 9.58 (offer price * debt / cash assumption) in cash for every share sold.

This can be checked easily as follows:

Offer price...

The cash per share and the exchange ratio is communicated to the selling shareholders in the offer document

Share information		
New shares issued	934.0	From Step 11
Buyer shares outstanding pre-deal	3,269.6	From Step 11
Target shares purchased	1,779.8	From Step 2
Exchange ratio - new for old	0.5248 x	BUY shares issued / TGT shares bought
Buyer DSO post-deal	4,203.6	From Step 11
% Buyer ownership post-deal	77.8%	BUY DSO / Combo DSO
% Target ownership post-deal	22.2%	TGT DSO / Combo DSO

Consideration per share check		
Offer price per share	**38.31**	From Step 1
Stock value per share	28.73	Exchange ratio * BUY share price
Cash per share	9.58	Offer price * % cash consideraton
Total value per share	**38.31**	Sum stock + cash value

So in this deal, the buyer has agreed to deliver 38.31 per share to the buyer and the current assumptions mean that this will be done by providing buyer shares worth 28.73 with 9.58 in cash.

Merger consequences analysis - contribution analysis

This takes key income statement / profit and loss metrics and calculates the proportion of the consolidated numbers going forward being provided or contributed by each of the parties. This can be compared with the percentage ownership of the combined entity and gives a view of the reasonableness of the offer compared to both parties contribution to the combined entity.

The analysis below is really useful as a negotiation tool especially when the deal is all equity financed. As in a normal contribution analysis, it compares the percentage contribution of key financial metrics (sales, EBIT etc) with the percentage ownership post deal. If these numbers do not align then a careful analysis of the logic of the proposed deal structure must be undertaken.

The percentage ownership is, of course, influenced by the relative valuation of the buyer and target. The analysis has been set up to be able to explore what happens to the numbers if the relative valuations vary. The model can select to use the buyer observed multiple or that of the target or a weighted average of both. An analysis of the variation in the results will force some challenging questions about relative valuation and the logic of the proposed deal structure.

Contribution Analysis

					% contribution			Implied Equity Ownership		Assumed Multiple
	Buyer	Target	Syn.	Combo	Buyer	Target	Syn.	Buyer	Target	Buyer
Sales										
XX H	87,906.0	46,018.4	0.0	133,924.4	65.6%	34.4%	0.0%	71.5%	28.5%	2.1 x
XY E	87,466.5	48,365.3	0.0	135,831.8	64.4%	35.6%	0.0%	70.0%	30.0%	2.1 x
XZ E	92,189.7	50,154.8	0.0	142,344.5	64.8%	35.2%	0.0%	70.5%	29.5%	2.0 x
EBITDA										
XX H	17,220.0	7,595.7	0.0	24,815.7	69.4%	30.6%	0.0%	76.1%	23.9%	10.6 x
XY E	17,143.4	8,222.1	100.0	25,465.5	67.3%	32.3%	0.4%	73.9%	26.1%	10.7 x
XZ E	18,069.2	8,777.1	200.0	27,046.3	66.8%	32.5%	0.7%	73.6%	26.4%	10.1 x
EBIT										
XX H	14,038.0	6,264.0	0.0	20,302.0	69.1%	30.9%	0.0%	75.8%	24.2%	13.0 x
XY E	13,983.7	6,662.0	100.0	20,745.8	67.4%	32.1%	0.5%	74.1%	25.9%	13.1 x
XZ E	14,691.9	7,186.6	200.0	22,078.5	66.5%	32.6%	0.9%	73.4%	26.6%	12.4 x
Net income										
XX H	10,267.0	3,067.1	0.0	13,334.1	77.0%	23.0%	0.0%	77.0%	23.0%	18.0 x
XY E	10,374.6	3,691.1	63.1	14,128.7	73.4%	26.1%	0.4%	73.8%	26.2%	17.3 x
XZ E	10,962.3	4,119.5	126.2	15,207.9	72.1%	27.1%	0.8%	72.7%	27.3%	16.3 x
Unaffected market cap.										
	179,010.7	52,448.9		231,459.6	77.3%	22.7%	0.0%	77.3%	22.7%	
Unaffected EV										
	182,864.7	76,991.3		259,856.1	70.4%	29.6%	0.0%			

Muliples Calculation	Buyer	Target	Weighted Average
EV/Sales			
XXH	2.1 x	1.7 x	2.0 x
XYE	2.1 x	1.6 x	1.9 x
XZE	2.0 x	1.5 x	1.9 x
EV/EBITDA			
XXH	10.6 x	10.1 x	10.5 x
XYE	10.7 x	9.4 x	10.3 x
XZE	10.1 x	8.8 x	9.7 x
EV/EBIT			
XXH	13.0 x	12.3 x	12.8 x
XYE	13.1 x	11.6 x	12.6 x
XZE	12.4 x	10.7 x	11.9 x
Price/Earnings			
XXH	18.0 x	16.5 x	17.7 x
XYE	17.3 x	14.2 x	16.6 x
XZE	16.3 x	12.7 x	15.5 x

Implied Value Calculations

	Implied Ex.	Implied EV		Implied Market Capitalization		Implied Share Price		WA Option Strike	
	Ratio	Buyer	Target	Buyer	Target	Buyer	Target	Buyer	Target
Sales									
XXH	0.731	182,864.7	95,728.8	179,010.7	71,186.4	54.75	40.02	18.4	21.9
XYE	0.785	182,864.7	101,116.6	179,010.7	76,574.2	54.75	42.98	18.4	21.9
XZE	0.769	182,864.7	99,485.7	179,010.7	74,943.2	54.75	42.08	18.4	21.9
EBITDA									
XXH	0.579	182,864.7	80,661.1	179,010.7	56,118.7	54.75	31.72	18.4	21.9
XYE	0.650	182,864.7	87,703.2	179,010.7	63,160.7	54.75	35.60	18.4	21.9
XZE	0.661	182,864.7	88,826.5	179,010.7	64,284.1	54.75	36.22	18.4	21.9
EBIT									
XXH	0.589	182,864.7	81,597.0	179,010.7	57,054.6	54.75	32.24	18.4	21.9
XYE	0.644	182,864.7	87,119.2	179,010.7	62,576.7	54.75	35.28	18.4	21.9
XZE	0.668	182,864.7	89,448.4	179,010.7	64,906.0	54.75	36.56	18.4	21.9
Net income									
XXH	0.552			185,164.5	55,314.0	56.63	31.28	18.4	21.9
XYE	0.655			179,010.7	63,688.7	54.75	35.89	18.4	21.9
XZE	0.691			179,010.7	67,269.7	54.75	37.86	18.4	21.9
Unaffected market cap.									
	0.538								

Merger consequences analysis - side by side comparison

This analysis lines up the key income statement / profit and loss performance indicators for both parties and is incredibly helpful when putting together a proposal that makes sense or for analyzing the relative strengths or weaknesses of a proposed deal structure.

Side by Side Comparison

	BUYER			Cagr	TARGET			Cagr	COMBO	
	XX H	XY E	XZ E	H - E	XX H	XY E	XZ E	H - E	XY E	XZ E
Sales	**87,906**	**87,466**	**92,190**	**2.4x**	**46,018**	**48,365**	**50,155**	**4.4x**	**135,832**	**142,345**
Growth %		(0.5%)	5.4%			5.1%	3.7%			4.8%
Gross profit	**43,131**	**42,953**	**45,191**	**2.4x**	**16,742**	**17,508**	**18,426**	**4.9x**	**60,411**	**63,568**
Growth %		(0.4%)	5.2%			4.6%	5.2%			5.2%
Margin %	49.1%	49.1%	49.0%		36.4%	36.2%	36.7%		44.5%	44.7%
Synergies	**nm**	**nm**	**nm**		**nm**	**nm**	**nm**		**100**	**200**
Growth %	nm	nm	nm		nm	nm	nm			100.0%
Margin %	nm	nm	nm		nm	nm	nm		0.1%	0.1%
EBITDA	**17,220**	**17,143**	**18,069**	**2.4x**	**7,596**	**8,222**	**8,777**	**7.5x**	**25,466**	**27,046**
Growth %		(0.4%)	5.4%			8.2%	6.7%			6.2%
Margin %	19.6%	19.6%	19.6%		16.5%	17.0%	17.5%		18.7%	19.0%
EBIT	**14,038**	**13,984**	**14,692**	**2.3x**	**6,264**	**6,662**	**7,187**	**7.1x**	**20,496**	**21,829**
Growth %		(0.4%)	5.1%			6.4%	7.9%			6.5%
Margin %	16.0%	16.0%	15.9%		13.6%	13.8%	14.3%		15.1%	15.3%
PBT	**12,120**	**14,403**	**15,236**	**12.1x**	**3,383**	**5,039**	**5,684**	**29.6x**	**18,266**	**19,790**
Growth %		18.8%	5.8%			49.0%	12.8%			8.3%
Margin %	13.8%	16.5%	16.5%		7.4%	10.4%	11.3%		13.4%	13.9%
Net income	**10,267**	**10,375**	**10,962**	**3.3x**	**3,067**	**3,691**	**4,119**	**15.9x**	**12,965**	**14,018**
Growth %		1.0%	5.7%			20.3%	11.6%			8.1%
Margin %	11.7%	11.9%	11.9%		6.7%	7.6%	8.2%		9.5%	9.8%
Cash EPS	**3.04**	**3.17**	**3.35**	**5.1x**	**1.78**	**2.07**	**2.31**	**13.9x**	**3.20**	**3.44**
Growth %		4.5%	5.7%			16.3%	11.6%			7.7%
Acc. / Dil.									0.7%	2.7%
Synergies to breakeven									212	0
Net debt	**3,854**	**179**	**(4,302)**	**na**	**24,542**	**23,927**	**22,504**	**(4.2x)**	**44,106**	**39,331**
Growth %		(95.4%)	(2501.8%)			(2.5%)	(5.9%)			(10.8%)
Net debt / EBITDA	0.22 x	0.01 x	(0.24)x		3.23 x	2.91 x	2.56 x		1.73 x	1.45 x

Merger consequences analysis - analysis at various prices

This is a key look-up table for use throughout the deal analysis. Any conversations will often revolve around offer price and this table summarizes the valuation impact of differing offer prices. Consequently, it should be immediately referenced when having discussions around pricing. As with all comparables, the value of this table of data is dependent on the use of appropriate benchmarks.

Look-up...

This table of data is invaluable as a quick reference for the impact of valuation changes

Analysis at Various Prices

Offer Price	Offer Prem.	Equity Value	Offer EV	EV/EBITDA LTM	EV/EBITDA XY E	EV/EBITDA XZ E	P/E XY E	P/E XZ E
29.47	0%	52,449	76,991	10.1 x	9.4 x	8.8 x	14.2 x	12.7 x
32.41	10%	57,694	82,236	10.8 x	10.0 x	9.4 x	15.6 x	14.0 x
35.36	20%	62,939	87,481	11.5 x	10.6 x	10.0 x	17.1 x	15.3 x
38.31	30%	68,184	92,726	12.2 x	11.3 x	10.6 x	18.5 x	16.6 x
41.26	40%	73,428	97,971	12.9 x	11.9 x	11.2 x	19.9 x	17.8 x
44.20	50%	78,673	103,216	13.6 x	12.6 x	11.8 x	21.3 x	19.1 x
47.15	60%	83,918	108,461	14.3 x	13.2 x	12.4 x	22.7 x	20.4 x
50.10	70%	89,163	113,706	15.0 x	13.8 x	13.0 x	24.2 x	21.6 x
53.04	80%	94,408	118,950	15.7 x	14.5 x	13.6 x	25.6 x	22.9 x
55.99	90%	99,653	124,195	16.4 x	15.1 x	14.1 x	27.0 x	24.2 x
58.94	100%	104,898	129,440	17.0 x	15.7 x	14.7 x	28.4 x	25.5 x
Trading Comps - Median				10.2 x	9.5 x	8.8 x	14.7 x	13.3 x
Transaction comps - Median				14.1 x	na	na	na	na
Buyer				10.6 x	10.7 x	10.1 x	17.3 x	16.3 x

Merger consequences analysis - return on invested capital - development over time

This is a calculation which compares the cost of the target with the incremental profits delivered by this target. The calculation must start with a definition of invested capital. This is the offer enterprise value plus the fees associated with the transaction. This gives the total investment in the acquisition of the target business.

This invested capital should be increased / decreased over time by the capital invested by the target. If this is not done a disconnect will arise, over time, between the target profits and the invested capital used to generate those profits.

The next step is to calculate the profit generated by the target. Here it is incremental profits to the buyer that needs to be considered. In principle, this is the profit provided by the target plus the synergies that are expected on integrating the target. These synergies are included as they are incremental cash flows generated by the deal.

Given invested capital is based on the enterprise value then the level of profit to be analyzed is EBIT after taxes - often referred to as net operating profit after taxes or NOPAT.

It should be noted that the tax rate to apply to the EBIT of the target is the expected effective tax rate (ETR) of the target. ETR must be used when taxing profits. If ETR and marginal tax rate (MTR) are approximately the same then practitioners often use MTR as a shortcut. In this case there is a significant difference between ETR and MTR and therefore it is material which tax rate is used in which calculation. When taxing the synergies, then MTR should be used since it is a marginal adjustment. Since the synergies are normally realized at the target then target MTR is typically used, however, the MTR should really follow the location of the synergy generation.

The return is calculated as follows:

$$\frac{\text{Incremental NOPAT}}{\text{Offer EV plus fees}}$$

Return on Invested Capital Analysis				
	XX H	XY E	XZ E	
Invested capital calculation				
Beginning invested capital		94,887.3	95,546.8	From last year
TGT capex		1,644.4	1,705.3	Forecast
TGT inc (dec) in OWC		244.9	7.2	Forecast
TGT D&A		(1,560.1)	(1,590.5)	Forecast
TGT (inc) dec other LTL		0.0	0.0	Forecast
TGT inc (dec) in other assets		330.2	62.6	Forecast
Ending invested capital	**94,887.3**	**95,546.8**	**95,731.3**	Sum
Net operating profit after-tax calculation				
Target EBIT		6,662.0	7,186.6	Forecast
Target effective tax rate		31.5%	31.5%	Forecast
Target NOPAT		**4,563.5**	**4,922.8**	EBIT * (1 - ETR)
Synergies pre-tax		100.0	200.0	Assumption
Target marginal tax rate		36.9%	36.9%	Assumption
Synergies post-tax		63.1	126.2	Assumption * (1- TGT MTR)
Adjusted NOPAT		**4,626.6**	**5,049.0**	TGT + post-tax synergies
Return on invested capital analysis				
Acquisition ROIC		**4.9%**	**5.3%**	(TGT NOPAT + syn.) / inv. cap
Buyer stand-alone		14.7%	15.2%	NOPAT / inv. cap.
Target stand-alone		7.8%	8.4%	NOPAT / inv. cap.
Combo		9.1%	9.6%	NOPAT / inv. cap.

Merger consequences analysis - premium analysis - development over time

This analysis focuses on the premium paid for the target and compares it to the expected benefit. Calculating the premium paid is relatively straightforward by comparing the unaffected market capitalization with the offer equity price.

Next the synergy calculation must be done. This is done on a post-tax basis, since the benefit is received post-tax. Also, once the run rate of synergies is achieved they will produce an annual benefit. This means that there is a disconnect being the premium being paid now with the benefit of the synergies which is realized annually into the future. This is solved by discounting the synergies which of course leads to the final issue for this calculation - which discount rate should be used.

A fundamental principle of discounting is that the discount rate must match the risk of the cash flows being discounted. This means that if the synergies are being realized at the target then it is the target risk that must be considered. Since synergies are always discussed at an operational level this means that the discount rate must take into account the return required from all providers of capital (both debt and equity). The weighted average cost of capital (normally the target) should be used. However, most would agree that there are special risk factors applied to the realization of synergies so that frequently a "risk factor" is added to the target WACC in recognition that these particular cash flows are more risky than the average cash flows of the target. Of course, it is impossible to calculate exactly what this "risk factor" should be. A sensitivity analysis should be undertaken to establish the impact of this assumption to the analysis.

It is also reasonable to mid-year adjust the valuation since the process of discounting assumes an "end of period" timing. This is very conservative since the synergies are actually being realized over the entire course of each year. A reasonable compromise is to assume that they are realized at the mid-point of the period.

Offer Premium Analysis	XX H	XY E....	...YD E	
Target unaffected market cap.	52,448.9			From step 3
Target equity purchase price	68,183.5			From step 3
Total premium paid	**15,734.7**			Difference
WACC	6.6%			Target WACC
Risk premium	2.0%			Estimate
Discount rate	8.6%			Sum
Pre-tax synergies		100.0	800.0	Assumption
Target marginal tax rate		36.9%	36.9%	Assumption
Post-tax synergies		63.1	504.8	Assumption * (1 - TGT MTR)
Terminal value			5,849.4	Perpetuity formula
Present value of synergies	1,365.4			Discounted
Present value of terminal value	3,559.7			Discounted
Total PV of synergies	4,925.0			Sum
Mid-year adjusted PV	**5,133.1**			PV * (1 + discount rate) ^0.5
Less premium paid	15,734.7			From above
Value created / (destroyed)	**(10,601.5)**			PV of synergies - premium

In this example, the present value of the synergies is a lot less than the premium being paid. It is important, when advising on a deal, that information, such as this, is considered, understood and evaluated.

Merger consequences analysis - credit analysis - including affordability of new financing structure

The credit implications of the proposed financing of the deal can be significant if the proposed leverage is high. This must be analyzed by calculating credit metrics. The goal, in this instance, is to identify whether the extra debt will cause a change in the credit rating. It also gives an indication of how easy it will be to sell this debt issuance to the market place (whether public or commercial bank debt). Below is a sample of credit metrics that might be calculated. Often, variants on the main metrics are calculated to take account of the specifics of a particular industry. Finally, the acceptable level of these metrics is driven by market sentiment.

Credit Analysis				
	XX H	XY E	XZ E	
BUYER				
EBITDA	17,220.0	17,143.4	18,069.2	Forecast
Net cash int. exp.	776.0	280.4	156.2	Forecast
Total net debt	3,854.0	179.1	(4,302.3)	Forecast
Net debt / EBITDA	**0.2 x**	**0.0 x**	**(0.2) x**	Net debt / EBITDA
EBITDA / net cash int. e	**22.2 x**	**61.1 x**	**115.7 x**	EBITDA / net cash int. exp.
COMBO				
EBITDA		25,465.5	27,046.3	Step 13
Net cash int. exp.		2,453.6	2,283.9	Step 14
Total net debt		43,527.4	38,848.8	Step 17
Net debt / EBITDA		**1.7 x**	**1.4 x**	Net debt / EBITDA
EBITDA / net cash int. exp.		**10.4 x**	**11.8 x**	EBITDA / net cash int. exp.

Merger modeling issues

Noncontrolling interests (NCI)

Noncontrolling shareholders (historically known as minority shareholders or minority interests) exist when the parent controls a subsidiary but does not own all of the equity of that business. In this case some of the equity funding of the group is provided by shareholders other than those who own the parent (the main shareholders). Noncontrolling shareholders own a part of a part of the group. This cannot be ignored.

Deal Funding	
Uses	
Price paid	250.0
Sources	
Debt raised	250.0

Equity Calculations		
TGT equity	222.0	TGT financials
% acquired	80.0%	% bought
Buyer share of TGT equity	177.6	% bought * TGT SE
% noncontrolling interest	20.0%	1 - % bought
NCI share of TGT equity	44.4	NCI % * TGT SE

When a NCI is created

A noncontrolling interest is created when a buyer achieves control of an entity but with less than 100% of the equity bought. At this stage the noncontrolling interest is calculated in two possible ways depending on which GAAP is being followed. Under IFRS, it is either:

- Noncontrolling shareholders' percentage of fair value of the shareholders' equity of the relevant subsidiary (called shareholder equity method from now on). This is straightforward to calculate. OR:
- Fair value of the noncontrolling interest (called fair value method from now on)

The fair value of the noncontrolling interest under the fair value method can be based on the share price, if there is one, or another valuation method such as trading comparables analysis. It should reflect a minority discount compared to the fair value per share of a controlling interest. The selected valuation method needs to be disclosed in the financial statements. This fair value exercise only occurs on the acquisition of the controlling interest by the parent and is not updated thereafter.

Under US GAAP, the only acceptable method for noncontrolling interest in the balance sheet is the fair value method.

This variation in methodology impacts both the NCI in the balance sheet (shown on the balance sheet in the equity section) and also the goodwill calculation. It is also only an implication at the deal date - going forward both methods calculate the noncontrolling interest in the same way but simply have a different starting point.

If the shareholder equity method is used then the implication is relatively straightforward. Ensure the percentage of shareholders' equity purchased is included (the NCI share is shown as NCI). This is the only adjustment required.

Goodwill - Shareholder Equity Method		
Price paid	250.0	From sources and uses
Buyer share of TGT equity	177.6	% bought * TGT SE
Goodwill	**72.4**	The difference

NCI...

Appears on the balance sheet as part of equity

	BUY Deal date	TGT Deal date	Deal Changes	Opening BS	
Cash	115.0	52.0		167.0	Buyer + Target
Other assets	470.0	265.0	72.4	807.4	BUY + TGT + new
Total Assets	**585.0**	**317.0**		**974.4**	
Liabilities	130.0	95.0	250.0	475.0	BUY + TGT + new
Equity	455.0	222.0	(222.0)	455.0	BUY + TGT - TGT
NCI	0.0	0.0	44.4	44.4	NCI % * Target SE
Total L&E	**585.0**	**317.0**		**974.4**	
Check	*OK*	*OK*		*OK*	

If the fair value method is used then a separate component must be added to the initial goodwill calculation. To start, do a standard goodwill calculation - this gives the goodwill attributable to the main shareholder. A secondary goodwill calculation then derives the goodwill attributable to NCI. This calculation takes the fair value less the NCI percentage of shareholders' equity. Total goodwill is made up of the goodwill attributable to all shareholders, including NCI.

Fair value method for goodwill...

This method calculates goodwill on a 100% stake and allocates a portion to the NCI

Goodwill - Fair Value Method		
Price paid	250.0	From sources and uses
Buyer share of TGT equity	177.6	% bought * TGT SE
Goodwill on buyer stake	**72.4**	The difference
FV of NCI	52.0	Using a valuation technique
NCI share of TGT equity	44.4	NCI % * Target SE
Goodwill on NCI stake	**7.6**	The difference
Total goodwill	**80.0**	Sum

	BUY Deal date	TGT Deal date	Deal Changes	Opening BS	
Cash	115.0	52.0		167.0	BUY + TGT
Other assets	470.0	265.0	80.0	815.0	BUY + TGT + new
Total Assets	**585.0**	**317.0**		**982.0**	
Liabilities	130.0	95.0	250.0	475.0	BUY + TGT + new
Equity	455.0	222.0	(222.0)	455.0	BUY + TGT - TGT
NCI	0.0	0.0	52.0	52.0	NCI fair value
Total L&E	**585.0**	**317.0**		**982.0**	
Check	*OK*	*OK*		*OK*	

Year on year - income statement / profit and loss

Include an extra line at the bottom of the income statement / profit and loss account called noncontrolling interest. This is calculated by taking their share of the net income / profit after tax of the relevant subsidiary. This divides the net income into the proportion attributable to the two groups of shareholders - the main shareholders (those of the parent) and the third party shareholders in any subsidiaries (noncontrolling interests).

NCI and the IS

The income statement / profit and loss account reports 100% but allocates net income into the two shareholder groups

COMBO

Income Statement	Hist.	Year 1	Year 2	
Revenues	170.0	290.0	320.0	BUY + TGT
Costs	(115.0)	(180.0)	(205.0)	BUY + TGT
Net income	**55.0**	**110.0**	**115.0**	
NI attributable to NCI	0.0	(8.0)	(8.0)	NCI % of TGT NI
NI attributable to parent shareholders	**55.0**	**102.0**	**107.0**	

Year on year - balance sheet

Noncontrolling interests are shareholders and like all shareholders they own shareholders' equity. Shareholders' equity goes up as the business earns profits and goes down as the business pays dividends. Since NCI is accounted for in a similar way to shareholders' equity, the NCI BASE analysis works in the same way.

COMBO - shareholder equity method for NCI

Balance Sheet	Hist.	Deal date	Year 1	Year 2	
Cash	70.0	167.0	202.0	247.0	From CFS
Other assets	450.0	807.4	962.4	1,052.4	BUY + TGT + new
Total Assets	**520.0**	**974.4**	**1,164.4**	**1,299.4**	
Liabilities	120.0	475.0	555.0	575.0	BUY + TGT + new
Equity	400.0	455.0	557.0	664.0	Beg. + NI - divis.
Noncontrolling interest	0.0	44.4	52.4	60.4	Beg. + NI - divis.
Total L&E	**520.0**	**974.4**	**1,164.4**	**1,299.4**	
Balance check	*OK*	*OK*	*OK*	*OK*	

BASE - NCI	Deal date	Year 1	Year 2	
Beginning amount		44.4	52.4	From BS
NI attributable to NCI		8.0	8.0	From IS
Dividends paid to NCI		0.0	0.0	From CFS
Ending amount	44.4	52.4	60.4	

Fair value method and NCI

The goodwill allocated to NCI changes only the starting number. Note that both BASE analyses are identical except for the starting point

COMBO - Fair value method for NCI

Balance Sheet	Hist.	Deal date	Year 1	Year 2	
Cash	70.0	167.0	202.0	247.0	From CFS
Other assets	450.0	815.0	970.0	1,060.0	BUY + TGT + new
Total Assets	**520.0**	**982.0**	**1,172.0**	**1,307.0**	
Liabilities	120.0	475.0	555.0	575.0	BUY + TGT + new
Equity	400.0	455.0	557.0	664.0	Beg. + NI - divis.
Noncontrolling interest	0.0	52.0	60.0	68.0	Beg. + NI - divis.
Total L&E	**520.0**	**982.0**	**1,172.0**	**1,307.0**	
Balance check	*OK*	*OK*	*OK*	*OK*	

BASE - NCI	Deal date	Year 1	Year 2	
Beginning amount		52.0	60.0	From BS
NI attributable to NCI		8.0	8.0	From IS
Dividends paid to NCI		0.0	0.0	From CFS
Ending amount	52.0	60.0	68.0	

Year on year - cash flow statement

The cash flow statement must show the net income to all the shareholders in the operating section and must show the dividends paid to all shareholders in the financing section. Typically this data is presented in 2 separate lines, for example, in the financing section, there will be a line called “Dividends paid” and another separate line called “Dividends paid to noncontrolling interests”.

The consolidated cash flow statement is built using the consolidated balance sheets and income statement / profit and loss account. This means that the cash flows of the subsidiary will automatically be included. There is an extra line item in the balance sheet and remember the cash flow is a reconciliation of the balance sheet so all balance sheet items must be included.

COMBO

Cash Flow Statement		Year 1	Year 2	
NI attributable to parent shareholders		102.0	107.0	From IS
NI attributable to NCI		8.0	8.0	From IS
Δ in other assets		(155.0)	(90.0)	From BS
Δ in liabilities		80.0	20.0	From BS
Δ in cash		**35.0**	**45.0**	
Opening cash		167.0	202.0	From BS
Closing cash	**167.0**	**202.0**	**247.0**	

Different year ends

If the buyer and target year ends are not coterminous, it is typical to adjust the target financials to align its year end with that of the buyer. This is done via a process of "calendarization". If the buyer has a December year end but that of the target is to June then to create a December year end for the target, 6 months worth of one year will be added to 6 months worth of the next year. This creates a pseudo December financial year for the target which can then easily be consolidated with that of the buyer.

In the illustration below the period from July 1st 2011 to Sept 30th 2011 is added to the period from Oct 1st 2011 to Jun 30th 2012. This creates a 12-month period to Jun 30th 2012. For example:

Sales to Sept 30th 2011 * 25.2% + Sales to Sept 30th 2012 * 74.8% = Sales to June 30th 2012

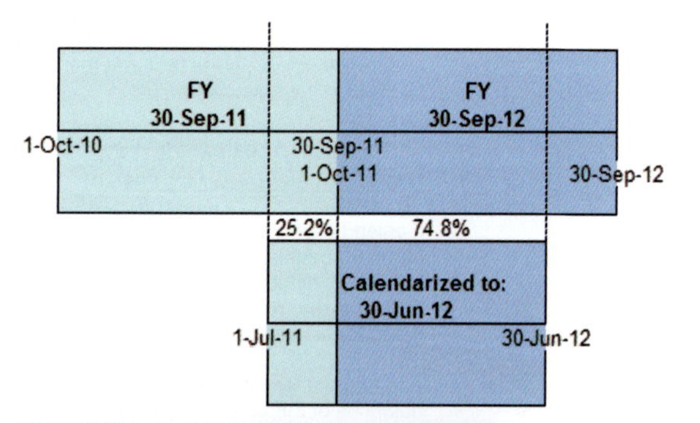

Calendarizing the target		
Buyer year-end	30-Jun-11	
Target year-end	30-Sep-11	
Days difference	**(92.0)**	From buyer to target

% of year	% Y-1	% Year	% Y+1	
	25.2%	74.8%	0.0%	MAX(Days difference / 365,0)
	MAX(- Days difference / 365,0)	Balance		

In the example above, the buyer year end is trailing that of the target which means the calendarization will take some of the current year numbers plus some of the prior year numbers. In other words, the calendarization is backwards in time.

If the target's year end is trailing that of the buyer then the calendarization will be forwards in time as illustrated below.

Calendarizing the target		
Buyer year-end	30-Sep-11	
Target year-end	30-Mar-11	
Days difference	**184.0**	From buyer to target

% of year	% Y-1	% Year	% Y+1	
	0.0%	49.6%	50.4%	MAX(Days difference / 365,0)
	MAX(- Days difference / 365,0)	Balance		

When building a model which going is to be used for many deals, this part of the model must be flexible so that it works regardless of which way around the dates fall. To do this use a base year and calculate what happens to base year +1 and base year -1. First calculate the days (or months) difference between the buyer and target dates. If the buyer is trailing the target this gives a negative number but if the target trails the buyer it will be positive. This value is then used to calculate the proportion of each year to be used. The calculation takes the days difference as a proportion of 365 (since this is an estimation process at best it is entirely unnecessary to worry about leap year issues).

For base year + 1 the formula is:

MAX (Days difference / 365,0)

If calendarizing backwards in time, days difference will be a negative number and this formula will return a value. If going forwards in time, days difference will be positive and the MAX function will ensure a zero result reflecting the fact that the forward period is not going to be used in the calculation.

For base year - 1, the formula is:

MAX (Days difference * - 1 / 365,0)

If calendarizing forward in time, days difference will be a positive number and this formula will return a value. If going backwards in time, days difference will be negative and the MAX function will ensure a zero result reflecting the fact that the forward period is not going to be used in the calculation.

The formula for the base year is 1 - (base +1 + base -1) or the balances of the proportion from 100%. So, in the example above, where the days difference is 184, the base year is 49.6% which is calculated as 1 - (50.4% + 0.0%).

There is one further implication of the calendarization process. This is caused by the fact that at one end of the time series the numbers produced will be meaningless because one of the two relevant period data sets is missing.

The problem period is normally obvious because the numbers will seem unreasonably small relative to the neighboring data sets. It is best to highlight this in some way, such as using conditional formatting or zero'ing out the affected numbers. Conditional formatting has been used in the cases below.

If you are calendarizing backwards in time the "problem" period will be the earliest in the time series (shaded below).

TARGET	30-Jun-10	30-Jun-11	30-Jun-12	30-Jun-13
Calendarization possible?	0	1	1	1
Income Statement				
Revenues	14,605.4	19,161.4	19,152.0	19,463.1
Operating expenses	(13,496.6)	(17,658.0)	(17,577.5)	(17,907.0)
EBIT	1,108.8	**1,503.4**	**1,574.5**	**1,556.1**
Interest inc/(exp)	(110.5)	(175.4)	(187.7)	(173.7)
PBT	998.2	**1,328.0**	**1,386.8**	**1,382.4**
Tax expense	(222.2)	(322.5)	(466.2)	(496.9)
Net income	776.0	**1,005.5**	**920.6**	**885.5**
Balance Sheet				
Cash	1,419.4	1,538.5	1,652.3	1,615.9
Other current assets	3,776.3	4,737.1	4,655.4	4,729.6
Goodwill	2,457.4	2,887.6	2,753.5	2,753.5
Other non-current assets	4,319.0	5,281.5	5,221.8	5,357.5
Total Assets	11,972.2	**14,444.7**	**14,283.0**	**14,456.5**
Debt	3,524.2	4,305.1	4,085.1	3,587.3
Other liabilities	5,319.5	6,810.3	6,731.4	6,797.7
Equity	3,128.5	3,329.3	3,466.6	4,071.5
Total L&E	11,972.2	**14,444.7**	**14,283.0**	**14,456.5**
Balance check	0.0	0.0	0.0	0.0
Cash flow statement				
Net income		1,005.5	920.6	885.5
Δ in Other current assets		(960.8)	81.7	(74.2)
Δ in Goodwill		(430.2)	134.1	0.0
Δ in Other non-current assets		(962.5)	59.7	(135.7)
Δ in Debt		780.8	(220.0)	(497.8)
Δ in Other liabilities		1,490.9	(78.9)	66.3
Dividends paid		(804.6)	(783.4)	(280.5)
Δ in Cash		119.1	**113.8**	**(36.4)**
Opening cash		1,419.4	1,538.5	1,652.3
Closing cash		1,538.5	**1,652.3**	**1,615.9**

On the other hand, if you are calendarizing forward in time, this will happen in the latest period in the time series (shaded below).

TARGET	30-Sep-10	30-Sep-11	30-Sep-12	30-Sep-13
Calendarization possible?	1	1	1	0

Income Statement				
Revenues	19,280.7	19,114.9	19,374.2	9,697.1
Operating expenses	(17,784.1)	(17,561.2)	(17,805.0)	(8,932.2)
EBIT	**1,496.6**	**1,553.7**	**1,569.1**	**765.0**
Interest inc/(exp)	(166.4)	(186.8)	(178.6)	(83.6)
PBT	**1,330.2**	**1,366.9**	**1,390.5**	**681.3**
Tax expense	(314.2)	(422.1)	(501.7)	(243.9)
Net income	**1,015.9**	**944.8**	**888.8**	**437.4**

Balance Sheet				
Cash	1,655.6	1,575.7	1,653.6	782.0
Other current assets	4,838.7	4,647.8	4,707.9	2,356.4
Goodwill	3,017.4	2,753.5	2,753.5	1,365.4
Other non-current assets	5,442.2	5,187.1	5,325.0	2,673.4
Total Assets	**14,954.0**	**14,164.1**	**14,440.0**	**7,177.3**
Debt	4,437.7	4,112.1	3,740.5	1,700.4
Other liabilities	6,908.7	6,724.0	6,778.6	3,380.7
Equity	3,607.5	3,328.1	3,921.0	2,096.2
Total L&E	**14,954.0**	**14,164.1**	**14,440.0**	**7,177.3**
Balance check	0.0	0.0	0.0	0.0

Cash flow statement				
Net income		944.8	888.8	437.4
Δ in Other current assets		191.0	(60.2)	2,351.5
Δ in Goodwill		263.9	0.0	1,388.1
Δ in Other non-current assets		255.1	(137.9)	2,651.5
Δ in Debt		(325.6)	(371.6)	(2,040.1)
Δ in Other liabilities		(184.7)	54.6	(3,397.9)
Dividends paid		(1,224.3)	(295.9)	(2,262.2)
Δ in Cash		**(79.9)**	**77.9**	**(871.6)**
Opening cash		1,655.6	1,575.7	1,653.6
Closing cash		**1,575.7**	**1,653.6**	**782.0**

A formula which can be copied across the time series should be used as follows:

This uses the base year percentage times the base year data plus year +1 percentage times year +1 date plus year -1 percentage times year -1 data. This is a typical application of the SUMPRODUCT function.

SUMPRODUCT(% of year for Y-1, Year and Year + 1, data for year for Y-1, Year and Y + 1)

Once the target financials have been calendarized in this way the rest of the modeling and analysis is as normal.

Deal date different to year end

If the deal date is inconsistent with the financial year end and this is modeled out, several issues will arise and care must be taken to do the necessary adjustments correctly. First, the deal date assumption should be documented along with the prior and following financial year end. This enables the calculation of the portion of the year that will elapse between the last year end and the deal date. In this model, this period of time is referred to as the roll forward period. Next the portion of the year between the deal date and the next year end should be calculated. In this model, this is called the stub period.

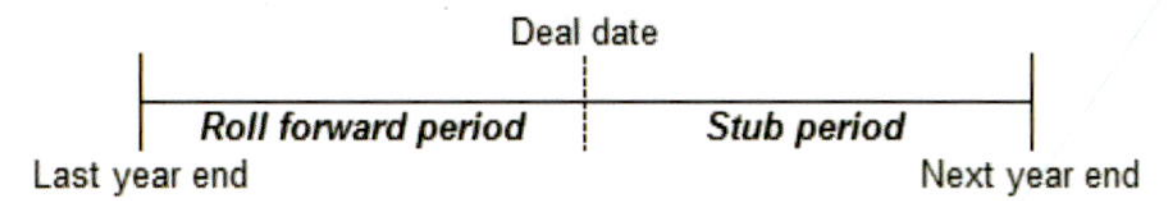

When doing the fundamental calculations necessary for merger analysis, problems arise. For example, when doing the goodwill calculation the net assets or shareholders' equity of the target at the deal date needs to drive the calculation. This will not be given by the last balance sheet or by the following forecast balance sheet. This problem is solved by the creation of a "deal date balance sheet".

Deal Date Calculations		
Deal date	25-Feb-12	
Buyer last year-end	30-Sep-11	
Buyer next year-end	30-Sep-12	
Stub %	**59.6%**	(Next ye - deal date) / (next ye - last ye)
Roll forward %	**40.4%**	1- stub%

There are two methods for the calculation of the deal date balance sheet:

- Roll forward and
- Calendarization

Roll forward method

The difference between the next year end and the last year end gives the change over the period. If it is assumed that this change arises evenly over the course of the year then the application of the roll forward period percentage will produce the amount of change from the last year end to the deal date. Adding this to the balance sheet amount from the last year end will produce an estimate of the balance at the deal date.

	Buyer Deal Date	Target Deal Date	
Cash	524.8	1,544.4	Last ye + roll forward% * (next ye - last ye)
Other current assets	2,795.5	4,644.7	Last ye + roll forward% * (next ye - last ye)
Goodwill	6,663.0	2,753.5	Last ye + roll forward% * (next ye - last ye)
Other NCA	7,717.7	5,172.9	Last ye + roll forward% * (next ye - last ye)
Total Assets	**17,701.0**	**14,115.5**	
Debt	6,541.5	4,123.1	Last ye + roll forward% * (next ye - last ye)
Other liabilities	5,401.3	6,721.0	Last ye + roll forward% * (next ye - last ye)
Equity	5,758.2	3,271.4	Last ye + roll forward% * (next ye - last ye)
Noncontrolling interest	0.0	0.0	
Total L&E	**17,701.0**	**14,115.5**	
Balance check	*0.0*	*0.0*	

Calendarization method

If the calendarization method is preferred then the last year end amount is apportioned by the stub period percentage and the next year end amount is multiplied by the roll forward period percentage and then these two values are summed.

	Buyer Deal Date	Target Deal Date	
Cash	524.8	1,544.4	Last ye * stub% + next ye * roll forward%
Other current assets	2,795.5	4,644.7	Last ye * stub% + next ye * roll forward%
Goodwill	6,663.0	2,753.5	Last ye * stub% + next ye * roll forward%
Other NCA	7,717.7	5,172.9	Last ye * stub% + next ye * roll forward%
Total Assets	**17,701.0**	**14,115.5**	
Debt	6,541.5	4,123.1	Last ye * stub% + next ye * roll forward%
Other liabilities	5,401.3	6,721.0	Last ye * stub% + next ye * roll forward%
Equity	5,758.2	3,271.4	Last ye * stub% + next ye * roll forward%
Noncontrolling interest	0.0	0.0	Last ye * stub% + next ye * roll forward%
Total L&E	**17,701.0**	**14,115.5**	
Balance check	*0.0*	*0.0*	

In each case the same result is achieved as can be seen from the example above (done both using each method in turn).

Once the deal date balance sheets are created then the proforma or opening balance sheet is completed normally with no hidden issues or complexities.

Equity Calculations		
Target equity	3,271.4	TGT financials @ deal date
% bought	80.0%	% bought
Target equity acquired	2,617.1	% bought * TGT SE @ deal date
% Noncontrolling interest	20.0%	1 - % bought
NCI created	654.3	NCI % * TGT SE @ deal date

Deal Funding	
Uses	
Price paid	6,000.0
Sources	
Equity issued	6,000.0

Goodwill Calculation		
Equity purchase price	6,000.0	From sources and uses
Target equity bought	2,617.1	% bought * TGT SE @ deal date
- Existing target goodwill	(2,753.5)	Revalue TGT goodwill, @ deal date, to zero
= FV of NAs purchased	(136.4)	
Goodwill	**6,136.4**	The difference

	Buyer Deal Date	Target Deal Date	Deal Changes	Opening BS	
Cash	524.8	1,544.4		2,069.2	BUY + TGT
Other current assets	2,795.5	4,644.7		7,440.2	BUY + TGT
Goodwill	6,663.0	2,753.5	3,382.9	12,799.4	BUY + TGT - TGT + new
Other NCA	7,717.7	5,172.9		12,890.6	BUY + TGT
Total Assets	17,701.0	14,115.5		**35,199.4**	
	0.0	0.0			
Debt	6,541.5	4,123.1		10,664.6	BUY + TGT
Other liabilities	5,401.3	6,721.0		12,122.3	BUY + TGT
Equity	5,758.2	3,271.4	2,728.6	11,758.2	
Noncontrolling interest	0.0	0.0	654.3	654.3	
Total L&E	17,701.0	14,115.5		**35,199.4**	
Balance check	0.0	0.0		*0.0*	

This is not the case when producing the consolidated income statement / profit and loss or cash flow statement going forward.

In the example shown below, the deal happens approximately half way through the middle year. This means that each of the three years shows are incomparable with each other. The earliest year is the buyer only. The middle year or deal year is the buyer plus the post deal portion of the target income statement / profit and loss. The latter year is the buyer plus the target. The latter year is the only set of formulae that can be copied forward in time.

To calculate the consolidated income statement / profit and loss in the deal year, the buyer numbers are added to the target numbers * the post deal portion of the period (in this case called the stub period percentage).

Watch out...

These three income statements/ profit and loss accounts are not comparable. The first has no target data included; the second has a portion included while the third has a full year included

Combo Income Statement	30-Sep-11	30-Sep-12	30-Sep-13	
Revenues	14,691.3	26,224.4	34,881.7	BUY + TGT * stub
Operating expenses	(12,298.7)	(22,702.2)	(30,597.2)	BUY + TGT * stub
EBIT	**2,392.6**	**3,522.2**	**4,284.5**	
Interest inc. / (exp.)	(390.0)	(449.2)	(468.3)	BUY + TGT * stub
PBT	**2,002.6**	**3,073.0**	**3,816.1**	
Tax expense	(720.4)	(1,088.6)	(1,349.6)	BUY + TGT * stub
Net income	**1,282.2**	**1,984.4**	**2,466.6**	
NI attributable to NCI	0.0	(106.7)	(176.4)	NCI % * TGT * stub
NI attributable to parent	**1,282.2**	**1,877.7**	**2,290.2**	

The consolidated balance sheet is produced in the normal way. The balance sheet is a point in time statement and consequently the date of the deal during the time period is irrelevant.

Combo Balance Sheet	30-Sep-11	30-Sep-12	30-Sep-13	
Cash	749.8	2,070.0	2,741.5	From CFS
Other current assets	2,785.1	7,474.1	7,664.0	BUY + TGT
Goodwill	6,663.0	12,799.4	12,799.4	BUY + TGT - TGT + new
Other NCA	7,676.9	13,035.5	13,375.7	BUY + TGT
Total Assets	**17,874.8**	**35,379.0**	**36,580.6**	
Debt	7,075.5	9,812.0	9,074.8	BUY + TGT
Other liabilities	5,382.3	12,168.5	12,442.3	BUY + TGT
Equity	5,417.0	12,637.5	14,126.1	RE BASE + new equity
Noncontrolling interest	0.0	761.0	937.4	BASE
Total L&E	**17,874.8**	**35,379.0**	**36,580.6**	
Balance check	*0.0*	*0.0*	*0.0*	

There are two methodologies possible for the cash flow statement. The first is to consolidate the standalone cash flows as with the income statement / profit and loss. For the deal year the target numbers will need to be apportioned such that only the post deal period is included. The application of the stub period percentage to the target cash flows will achieve this.

A step change in the cash flow happens on the deal date and this must be included in the investing activities section of the consolidated cash flow statement. This item shows the cash impact of the deal and is calculated by taking the cash consideration less any target cash acquired at the deal date. In this example, there is no cash consideration so the investing cash flow shows a positive (or inflow) of cash from the acquisition of the target's balance sheet cash at the deal date.

Combo Cash Flow	30-Sep-12	30-Sep-13	
NI attributable to parent	1,877.7	2,290.2	From combo IS
NI attributable to NCI	106.7	176.4	From combo IS
Δ in other current assets	(44.4)	(189.9)	BUY + TGT * stub
Δ in other liabilities	65.2	273.8	BUY + TGT * stub
Operating cash flows	**2,005.2**	**2,550.5**	
Δ in other NCA	(185.7)	(340.2)	BUY + TGT * stub
Business acquisition	1,544.4	0.0	Cash spent - TGT deal date cash
Investing cash flows	**1,358.7**	**(340.2)**	
Δ in debt	(1,386.6)	(737.3)	BUY + TGT * stub
Dividends paid	(657.2)	(801.6)	Assumption
Financing cash flows	**(2,043.8)**	**(1,538.8)**	
Δ in cash	**1,320.2**	**671.6**	
Opening cash	749.8	2,070.0	Beginning combo cash
Closing cash	**2,070.0**	**2,741.5**	Ending combo cash

Commonly, the cash flow statement is calculated by taking the change in the balance sheet numbers between one year end and the next. This will not work if the deal happens during the year. This is because the last year end balance sheet is represented by the buyer alone whereas the next year end balance sheet is made up of the buyer and target. If the change were to be taken to the cash flow statement in the "normal way", it assumes that the target balance sheet amount at the last year end was zero. This is solved by taking the beginning buyer amount plus the target deal date amount into the "change" calculation. The cash flows associated with the buyer for the full year and that of the target post deal are thus calculated.

Combo Cash Flow	30-Sep-12	30-Sep-13	
NI attributable to parent	1,877.7	2,290.2	From combo IS
NI attributable to NCI	106.7	176.4	From combo IS
Δ in other current assets	(44.4)	(189.9)	(BUY beg. + TGT @deal date) - combo end.
Δ in other liabilities	65.2	273.8	Combo end. - (BUY beg. + TGT @deal date)
Operating cash flows	**2,005.2**	**2,550.5**	
Δ in other NCA	(185.7)	(340.2)	(BUY beg. + TGT @deal date) - combo end.
Business acquisition	1,544.4	0.0	Cash spent - TGT deal date cash
Investing cash flows	**1,358.7**	**(340.2)**	
Δ in debt	(1,386.6)	(737.3)	Combo end. - (BUY beg. + TGT @deal date)
Dividends paid	(657.2)	(801.6)	Assumption
Financing cash flows	**(2,043.8)**	**(1,538.8)**	
Δ in cash	1,320.2	671.6	
Opening cash	749.8	2,070.0	Beginning combo cash
Closing cash	**2,070.0**	**2,741.5**	Ending combo cash

Goodwill and asset step-ups

Goodwill and taxes

When a business is interested in buying another business it can gain control by buying the equity (an equity deal) or by buying all the individual assets and liabilities instead (an asset deal). The latter might be more attractive, for example, to specifically exclude some of the liabilities of the target from the transaction.

There is no difference in the consolidated numbers reported between an asset or equity deal. The purpose of consolidated accounts is to show the underlying economics of the situation and to bypass the legal details. This also has no impact on taxes because most of the time the consolidated numbers are ignored for the purposes of calculating tax liabilities. However, the legal nature of the transaction (asset or equity deal) does impact the financials of the legal entity which bought the asset (the parent) and this often does have an impact on the tax treatment. This is subtle and given that in most countries the financials of the parent are not even published (just the consolidated financials) it is often not obvious what is driving the variation in taxation treatments.

Goodwill and taxes - an equity deal

Taxation is usually driven by the financials of the parent and not by the consolidated financials so in order to understand the taxation issues here, the treatment of the asset must be understood both in the consolidated financials and in the financials of the parent.

If the parent buys the equity of another company then, in the parent balance sheet, this is simply reported as a financial investment at cost. The cost is not broken down into the component parts (assets, liabilities and goodwill) as happens in the consolidated balance sheet. As a direct consequence of this no goodwill is recognized in the parent balance sheet.

Since the parent financials drive the taxation impact, no goodwill is recognized in the tax return and consequently no goodwill amortization is tax deductible. This means that, although in most countries goodwill amortization is tax deductible, in fact, it is not deductible on equity deals simply because no goodwill is recognized in the parent's standalone balance sheet.

The goodwill is recognized on the consolidated balance sheet but this is not typically the driver of tax treatment and so is often irrelevant for taxes.

Goodwill and taxes - an asset deal

Remember, taxation is usually driven by the financials of the parent and not by the consolidated financials so in order to understand the taxation issues here, the treatment of the asset must be understood both in the consolidated financials and in the financials of the parent.

If the parent buys the net assets of another company then, in the parent balance sheet, this is reported by recording all the detailed assets and liabilities purchased. Since it is likely that a premium above book was paid then this too must be recorded in order for the balance sheet to balance. This means that goodwill is recorded in the parent's balance sheet directly and since this is the primary reporting entity for taxes it also stands that this goodwill may qualify for tax amortization.

Needless to say tax deductibility of goodwill is potentially very valuable for the buyer so it begs the question: Why are deals not always done like this and structured as asset deals? In fact, generally speaking, asset deals are tax advantageous for the buyer (for the reasons outlined) but are tax disadvantageous to the seller. In other words, buyers often like asset deals but sellers often do not.

It is also worth noting that the value of goodwill calculated for tax purposes may be different to that calculated for accounting purposes as tax rules differ to accounting rules.

Goodwill and taxes summary - for equity deals

In the consolidated financials (which we are concerned with):

Goodwill is not usually amortized for GAAP or tax purposes. Therefore there is no difference between GAAP and tax reporting, and consequently it can be ignored when calculating tax expense, taxes payable and deferred tax balances.

So if modeling an equity deal (most common) there are no tax implications of the creation of the goodwill asset in the consolidated balance sheet.

Goodwill and taxes summary - for asset deals

In the consolidated financials (which we are concerned with):

Goodwill is not amortized for GAAP purposes but may be amortized for tax reporting. This means that there is a difference between GAAP amortization (zero) and tax amortization (often over 15 years). This is considered to be a timing difference since the GAAP goodwill may be expensed in the income statement / profit and loss if an impairment is recognized in the future or on the eventual sale of the business. Depending on the GAAP, a deferred tax asset or liability may need to be recognized on the difference between GAAP goodwill and tax goodwill. The tax rules in this area are complex and the advice of a specialist should be sought if needed.

So if modeling an asset deal (less common) there are likely to be tax implications of the creation of the goodwill asset in the consolidated balance sheet and a deferred tax asset or liability may need to be created. This is most likely to be a deferred tax liability created over the tax deductible life of the goodwill amortization and reversing in the event of an impairment or the sale of the equity in question. Interestingly, neither of these "reversal events" are likely to be forecast in a merger model so the deferred tax will not reverse over the forecast period.

Asset step-ups and taxes

A similar problem arises as a result of an issue associated with goodwill. It is to do with the stepping up of assets when you do a fair value adjustment in order to calculate goodwill. Again, the tax authorities are primarily concerned with the legal entities rather than the consolidated financials. Once again, the main driver of the matter is the legal structure of the deal and whether the purchase of the equity of the target or the assets / liabilities of the target.

The key issue here is that if the assets are stepped up then the basis for calculating depreciation has increased and so will depreciation expense. So the question becomes whether the new asset basis is recognized for tax purposes or not. This is important because an increased tax depreciation schedule is clearly valuable to the buyer.

Asset step-ups and taxes - an equity deal

Here the target's equity is bought from the target's shareholders. From a legal viewpoint (and hence tax viewpoint) the ownership of the assets have not been transferred (before the deal they were owned by the target and after the deal they are still owned by the target) so therefore there is no change in legal status and consequently no change in tax basis. As a result, the depreciation and amortization schedule remains unchanged for tax purposes.

Asset step-ups and taxes - an asset deal

Here the assets have legally changed hands. Pre-deal they were owned by the target and post-deal they are owned by the buyer. The question is what amount the buyer paid for this particular asset. To figure this out the purchase price (for the whole business) must be divided into its component parts and this is gives the value of the assets at their stepped up amount. From a tax perspective, the ownership has changed and this drives a change to the tax basis. The stepped up value is the new tax basis, which means that higher tax depreciation and amortization expense will accrue.

Asset step-ups and taxes summary - for equity deals

In the consolidated financials (which we are concerned with):

The assets are stepped up for GAAP purposes and increased depreciation expense arises. The assets are not stepped up for tax reporting so no extra tax depreciation arises. This causes an extra difference between GAAP and tax reporting which must be reflected by extra deferred tax. The extra deferred tax liability is calculated as follows:

Step-up * tax rate = Extra deferred tax liability

This deferred tax liability will decrease each period as the extra depreciation tracks through the income statement / profit and loss account.

So, in an equity deal situation, if you step up the assets as part of the goodwill calculation, you must also include the deferred tax impact of the step-up and reverse the deferred tax liability as the step-up is depreciated.

Asset step-ups and taxes summary - for asset deals

The assets are stepped up for GAAP purposes and increased depreciation expense arises. The assets are also stepped up for tax reporting and therefore extra tax depreciation arises too. This means that the difference between GAAP and taxes is the same as it was pre-deal. Consequently there are no implications on the reported tax numbers and the step-ups can be ignored when calculating tax expense, taxes payable and deferred taxes.

So, in an asset deal situation, if you step up the assets as part of the goodwill calculation, there will be no deferred tax impact.